THE
BIBLE
BLUEPRINT

Other Loyola Press books by Joe Paprocki

A Well-Built Faith: A Catholic's Guide
to Knowing and Sharing What We Believe

A Well-Built Faith: A Leader's Guide

The Catechist's Toolbox: How to Thrive
as a Religious Education Teacher

The Catechist's Toolbox: A Leader's Guide

La caja de herramientas del catequista:
Cómo triunfar en el ministerio de la catequesis

La caja de herramientas del catequista:
Guía para el líder

Living the Mass:
How One Hour a Week Can Change Your Life
(with Fr. Dominic Grassi)

JOE PAPROCKI

THE
BIBLE
BLUEPRINT

A Catholic's Guide to Understanding and Embracing God's Word

LOYOLA PRESS.
A JESUIT MINISTRY
Chicago

LOYOLA PRESS.
A JESUIT MINISTRY

3441 N. Ashland Avenue
Chicago, Illinois 60657
(800) 621-1008
www.loyolapress.com

Portions of this book were previously published in *God's Library: A Catholic Introduction to the World's Greatest Book* (Chicago: Loyola Press, 2005) and in *God's Library: Introducing Catholics to the Bible* (Mystic, CT: Twenty-Third Publications, 1999).

In accordance with c. 827, permission to publish is granted on April 30, 2009 by the Very Reverend John F. Canary, Vicar General of the Archdiocese of Chicago. Permission to publish is an official declaration of ecclesiastical authority that the material is free from doctrinal and moral error. No legal responsibility is assumed by this grant of permission.

Cover and interior design: Tracy Sainz and Becca Gay
Cartoons: Copyright © Doug Hall, 1991. Used by Permission.

Unless otherwise noted, Scripture quotations are from New Revised Standard Version Bible: Catholic Edition, copyright © 1989, 1993 National Council of the Churches of Christ in the United States of America. Used by permission. All rights reserved.

Scripture quotations marked "NAB" are from the *New American Bible with Revised New Testament and Psalms*, Copyright © 1991, 1986, 1970 by the Confraternity of Christian Doctrine, Washington, DC. Used with permission. All rights reserved. No part of the *New American Bible* may be reproduced in any form without permission in writing from the copyright owner.

Excerpts from "The Interpretation of the Bible in the Church" (pp.78–80) by the Pontifical Biblical Commission are used by permission from Libreria Editrice Vaticana.

Library of Congress Cataloging-in-Publication Data
Paprocki, Joe.
    The Bible blueprint : a Catholic's guide to understanding and embracing God's Word / Joe Paprocki.
        p. cm.
    Rev. ed. of: God's library.
    Includes bibliographical references.
    ISBN-13: 978-0-8294-2898-8;   ISBN-10: 0-8294-2898-4
    1. Bible--Introductions. 2. Catholic Church--Doctrines. I. Paprocki, Joe. God's library.
II. Title.
    BS475.3.P35 2009
    220.6'1024282--dc22
                                                2009001455

Printed in the United States of America
09 10 11 12 13 RRD 10 9 8 7 6 5 4 3 2 1

DEDICATION

I dedicate this book to the late Sr. Georgine Smolinski, C.R., who firmly believed that a teenager could possibly be interested in the Bible, and to Fr. Terry Baum, SJ, for giving that teenager spiritual direction that has lasted a lifetime.

CONTENTS

ACKNOWLEDGMENTS

I would like to thank Pat Kahl for inviting me (back before the turn of the century) to do my first Bible workshop with her sixth graders and catechists at St. Terrence in Alsip, Illinois. From that point on, I have done dozens of Bible workshops for kids and adults all over the United States. It was from these workshops that I eventually developed a book titled *God's Library*, published first by Twenty-Third Publications and most recently by Loyola Press. The huge success of my books *The Catechist's Toolbox* and *A Well-Built Faith* convinced us at Loyola Press that we had identified a formula that speaks to the needs of the average Catholic. When it came time for a reprint of *God's Library*, it was a no-brainer to refine the work, update it, and present it as *The Bible Blueprint*. I would like to thank all of the countless people along the way who have inspired me to continue fine-tuning this work, most recently, Joe Durepos, Matthew Diener, Bret Nicholaus, Miguel Arias, Tom McGrath, Santiago Cortés-Sjöberg, and Steve Connor.

Special thanks to the many Scripture professors at whose feet I was privileged to sit, especially: Mark Link, SJ; Dr. Robert Ludwig; Dianne Bergant, C.S.A.; Donald Senior, C.P.; Barbara Reid, O.P.; Eugene LaVerdiere, S.S.S.; Leslie Hoppe, O.F.M.; Carroll Stuhlmueller, C.P.; Carolyn Osiek, R.S.C.J.; James McIlhone; John Lodge; and Robert Schoenstene. Special thanks also to some very talented Scripture scholars who I am blessed to call friends: Dr. Michael Cameron, Dr. James Campbell, and Tom McLaughlin.

Chapter One

Discovering the Bible Blueprint

You don't have to be an architect to understand the concept of a blueprint. Simply put, a blueprint is a plan. When a blueprint is followed properly, the result is a new creation. God has a plan for us, and, when we follow that plan, we become a new creation. The blueprint for salvation is found in the Bible, and the Bible itself is constructed according to a plan. Welcome to The Bible Blueprint!

Sitting above my desk at work is a painting of my patron saint, Joseph the carpenter, doing what we tend to associate with the role of a carpenter—carving wood. In fact, it's quite common for us to see images of the child Jesus carving wood as his earthly father, Joseph the carpenter, looks on. We tend to conclude that carpenters, in those days, were makers of "tables, chairs, and oaken chests" (as described in the song "Heaven on Their Minds" from *Jesus Christ Superstar*). In truth, during the time of Jesus, a carpenter was not merely a cabinetmaker but was comparable to an architect: someone who was skilled at designing buildings. It makes perfect sense that Jesus' earthly father, Joseph, was an architect since his heavenly Father is the "architect" of all creation.

Plain and simple, an architect is someone who designs a detailed plan—a blueprint.

For in the sacred books, the Father who is in heaven meets His children with great love and speaks with them; and the force and power in the word of God is so great that it stands as the support and energy of the Church, the strength of faith for her sons, the food of the soul, the pure and everlasting source of spiritual life. (*Dei Verbum*, 21)

God, indeed, is an architect with a plan:

> For surely I know the plans I have for you, says the LORD, plans
> for your welfare and not for harm, to give you a future with hope.
> (Jeremiah 29:11)

God's plan for us is no secret. He has provided us with a blueprint for our salvation: the Paschal Mystery—the suffering, death, and resurrection—of Jesus Christ. And where do we find this blueprint laid out for us? In the Bible.

So, just what is the Bible and how is it a blueprint for our salvation? Let's explore.

Jesus the Architect?

When the Bible refers to Jesus as a *carpenter* (Mark 6:3) and as the *carpenter's* son (Matthew 13:55), it uses the Greek word *tekton* which suggests not only a worker in wood but a builder. It should come to us as no surprise then, that Jesus uses the imagery of *building* quite freely in the Gospels:

- On this rock I will build my church . . . (Mt 16:18)
- The stone that the builders rejected
  has become the cornerstone . . . (Mt 21:42)
- I am able to destroy the temple of God and to build it in
  three days. (Mt 26:61)
- That one is like a man building a house, who dug deeply,
  and laid the foundation upon rock . . . (Lk 6:48)
- I will pull down my barns and build larger ones . . . (Lk 12:18)
- For which of you, intending to build a tower . . . (Lk 14:28)

The Bible Blueprint

While it is great to know that the Bible is a blueprint for our salvation, it is also helpful to know how to read blueprints. I recall years ago, when my dad was making plans to open a new family pharmacy to replace the old one that was being demolished, he had a set of blueprints drawn up for the new store. Although I couldn't make heads or tails of them, I was amazed at how various construction workers and electricians were able to glance at those blueprints and know exactly where to install a new store fixture or an electrical outlet. In a similar way, we need to be able to read God's blueprint for salvation as revealed in the Bible. The nice thing is, the Bible itself has a blueprint of sorts: a plan for its own arrangement. Here's what it looks like:

Old Testament	Catalog	New Testament
Pentateuch (Torah)	Table of Contents	Gospels
History		Acts
Wisdom		Letters
Prophets		Revelation

In fact, I find it helpful to carry this image of a blueprint even further and to think of the Bible as a building—a library, actually. I call it God's Library. If the Bible were indeed a building, then the above blueprint reveals to us how it is arranged. In short, we find the following:

- God's Library has two wings: an Old Testament wing and a New Testament wing.

- Both wings of the building are divided into four smaller stack rooms.

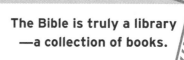

The Bible is truly a library —a collection of books.

- In the Old Testament wing, which is more than twice the size of the New Testament wing, we can find rooms dedicated to the Pentateuch, History, Wisdom, and the Prophets.

- In the New Testament wing, we can find rooms housing the Gospels, Acts of the Apostles, the Letters, and Revelation.

- There is also a foyer or front desk housing the card catalog or Table of Contents.

Of course, no such building exists. However, the Bible is truly a library—a collection of books. This metaphor can help us understand how to approach the Bible and, like an architect or construction worker, be capable of reading the blueprints and understanding how it will lead us to encounter God.

The Bible: What Is It?

Some years ago, Pepsi ran a television commercial that took place in a futuristic setting with a professor leading a group of students on an archeological dig. As they all drink from their Pepsi cans, one of them unearths a find; an object caked over with centuries of mud and dirt. Unable to make out what the object is, the professor places it in a device that quickly removes all of the layers of dirt, only to reveal an empty bottle of Coca-Cola. With puzzled expressions, the students look at the object and ask the professor, "What is it?" The professor, with the same puzzled expression, tilts the bottle this way and that before responding, "I have no idea!"—a clever poke at Coca-Cola.

> We receive far more than instruction from the Bible: we receive an invitation to an intimate relationship with the Creator of the universe.

When we encounter the Bible, the very first question we should ask is, "What is it?" and we need to come away with a much better answer than, "I have no idea." So, just what is the Bible?

First, when it comes to describing what the Bible is, I would like to lay to rest a cute acronym

B-asic
I -nstruction
B-efore
L-eaving
E-arth

Now, I know this acronym is likeable and there's nothing erroneous about it, but it does a disservice to the Bible. Yes, the Bible contains instruction; however, the Bible is much more than an instruction manual. Instruction manuals don't bring readers into intimate relationship with the books' authors. The Bible does. We receive far more than instruction from the Bible: we receive an invitation to an intimate relationship with the Creator of the universe.

Even better than an acronym for the Bible is one word that summarizes what the Bible is: *revelation*.

Now, I know that at first glance that word sounds deeply theological. It is not. The root word of revelation is, of course, the word *reveal*. Revelation occurs when someone or something is revealed. We humans know that revealing ourselves to others is the key to any relationship. When we meet someone for the first time, we exchange basic information about where we live, what we do for a living, who we live with, where we grew up, where we went to school, and so on. Why? To establish a relationship. The deeper we want the relationship to go, the more we reveal. If we don't want the relationship to go any further, we continue to talk about the weather.

So, the Bible is basically the record of God's revelation of himself to us. Why would God do this? To enter into a relationship with us. The Bible is an invitation to intimacy with God. If the Bible were solely an instruction manual, we could read it and still not know God. In reality, the Bible is one of the most crucial ways that we come to know God. Remember that for the Jewish people, the verb *to know* suggested intimacy (for example, Mary responding to the angel's announcement of her pregnancy by asking, "How can this be, since I do not know a man?" [Luke 1:34, NKJV]). By reading the Bible, we enter into a more intimate relationship with God who reveals himself to us throughout salvation history, culminating in the Incarnation of Jesus—the Word made flesh.

> **"Fight truth decay—study the Bible daily!"**
> —C. S. Lewis

We don't read the Bible to find answers. We don't study the Bible in order to be able to debate others about its meaning. When all is said and done, we *pray* the Bible so that we may encounter the living God who is revealing himself to us from Genesis 1:1 to Revelation 22:21.

A New Acronym?

Perhaps a better acronym for
B.I.B.L.E. would be the following:
B-lessed
I -ntimacy
B-egets
L-ife
E-verlasting

It is through an intimate relationship with the God of love that we find everlasting life!

Scripture and Tradition

The Word of God takes the form of both the written word (Scripture) and of a living Tradition. For Catholics, Scripture and Tradition are inseparable, forming one "sacred deposit of the Word of God" (*Catechism of the Catholic Church,* 97). Some people like to think that the Bible is the final word on all matters. There's only one problem with that. The Bible, as we know it today, is the product of Tradition. In other words, an oral tradition of preaching the Gospel existed before the New Testament was written down. Likewise, the final arrangement of the books of the Bible as we have it today was set in place by the leaders of the early Church. The Bible, which flows from Church Tradition, is part of a single source of God's revelation. It is the revealed Word of God.

Blueprints and Libraries: Why Use Metaphors?

Not all people need metaphors to grow in their understanding of the Bible. However, in my experience as a teacher, I have found that people, young and old, tend to learn more effectively when metaphors are employed in the process. Personally, I developed this blueprint/library metaphor almost thirty years ago when teaching high school religion in Chicago. I discovered early on that my freshman students were fairly clueless when it came to the Bible. Although the designated topic for freshmen was the sacraments, I asked my chairman if I could set aside one week to do a crash course on the Bible, which he agreed to.

I realized that the Bible as a whole was just too huge and that the students needed it to be broken down into bite-size pieces. Lo and behold, the arrangement of the Bible itself provided me with the clue I needed to help my students. Noticing that the table of contents for most Bibles arranged the Old Testament according to the categories of Pentateuch, History, Wisdom, and Prophets, and the New Testament according to Gospels, Acts of the Apostles, Letters, and Revelation, the image of a blueprint for a library building quickly entered my mind.

I immediately set out to work and created a cardboard model of a library building and called it God's Library. The building reflected the blueprint pictured earlier in this chapter. Next, I created bookmarks for the students—one for each of the eight sections of the Bible. Each bookmark included a brief overview of a particular section of the Bible along with a bulleted list of highlights to be found in each section. Using these bookmarks, I embarked on a crash course with my students designed to dramatically increase their knowledge of the Bible. At the end of the week, I invited my department chair to come to my class and invited him to call out the name of any famous Bible character, guaranteeing that the majority of my students would find a passage related to that character in under a minute. Thankfully, they were able to do so, and I kept my job!

"I Don't Know Anything about the Bible!"

It was not long thereafter that a DRE friend of mine invited me to come to her parish to do a shortened version of this activity with her sixth-grade religious education students. Over the next few years, I did dozens of these Bible workshops for students in religious education programs. I soon began to notice a pattern. At each event, the catechists who were present would come up to me afterward and tell me how much they enjoyed it, how much they thought it would help the kids, and how much they learned themselves. They would often say, "I don't know anything about the Bible . . . this really helped me." More and more I realized that adult Catholics were hungry for greater knowledge of the Bible. I began doing the presentations for groups of adults and eventually wrote the book *God's Library* to address this need in the Church. Now, some thirty years after this concept evolved out of a high school religion class, I offer you this basic introduction to the Bible—*The Bible Blueprint: A Catholic's Guide to Understanding and Embracing God's Word.* I hope you enjoy it and come to know our Lord more deeply through his Sacred Word in Scripture.

Ralph Gringer was the first to recognize that the new youth Bible study had created attitude problems.

SOME FOURTEEN-YEAR-OLD *PUNK* JUST QUOTED SCRIPTURE TO ME!

So, What's Stopping Us?

If the Bible is indeed a blueprint for how we can enter into a deeper, more intimate relationship with our loving God, what's stopping us from plunging headlong into its pages? Well, the fact is, we seem to have lots of reasons for keeping the Bible at arm's length. In the next chapter, we'll address these obstacles and begin to lay the foundation for overcoming them.

Questions for Reflection and Discussion

- How can it help us to approach the Bible by comparing it to a blueprint? a library?

- What is an example of a passage or story from the Bible that you find difficult to comprehend?

- With which of the eight sections of God's Library (Pentateuch, History, Wisdom, Prophets, Gospels, Acts of the Apostles, Letters, Revelation) are you most familiar? least familiar?

- Why is it not sufficient to say that the Bible is Basic Instruction Before Leaving Earth?

- Can you think of a time when you came to know someone more intimately because of something they had written (in a card or letter)? How can such examples help us to understand how we can become more intimate with God through Scripture reading?

- What is *revelation* and what does it have to do with the Bible?

- What do we mean by Church *Tradition*? How would you explain the relationship between Scripture and Tradition?

There was this gracious lady mailing an old family Bible to her brother in another part of the country. "Is there anything breakable in here?" asked the postal clerk. "Only the Ten Commandments," answered the lady.

Chapter Two

Overcoming "Bibliaphobia"

For many, trying to read blueprints is like learning a new language. Filled with abbreviations, signs, and symbols, a blueprint can intimidate even the brightest of minds. And yet, learning to read blueprints can be done without any formal schooling. For many of us, reading and understanding the Bible can be intimidating. Even when reading a Bible in our own language, we sometimes conclude, "It's like Greek to me." However, just as you don't have to be an architect to understand a blueprint, you don't have to be a Scripture scholar to understand the Bible.

In the famous cartoon *A Charlie Brown Christmas*, Charlie seeks the advice of his friend Lucy, explaining that he just doesn't feel right. Charlie listens as Lucy goes through a long list of phobias that might possibly explain Charlie's problem, including fears of responsibility, cats, staircases, the ocean, and crossing bridges. Finally, Lucy suggests that perhaps Charlie's problem is being caused by something called pantophobia. When Lucy explains that pantophobia is the fear of *everything*, Charlie shouts, "That's it!"

> Easy access to Sacred Scripture should be provided for all the Christian faithful. (*Dei Verbum*, 22)

The truth is that most of us have some sort of fear. Hopefully, you do not suffer from pantophobia, but many things about life can indeed be frightening. Two of the most common fears that people admit to are a fear of public speaking followed by a fear of death. Comedian Jerry Seinfeld points out how ironic it is that most of us have a greater fear of speaking at a funeral than we have of being the deceased person spoken of!

While surveys routinely reveal peoples' greatest fears, one fear often goes unnoticed. It is a fear that is common among Catholics. I call it *bibliaphobia,* or fear of the Bible. As Catholics, many of us were told that when it came to the idea of reading or studying the Bible, we should let Father explain it to us on Sunday. Even though Vatican II stressed the importance of becoming familiar with the Bible by reading and reflecting on the Scriptures on our own, it has been hard to shake the notion that Scripture study was something that Protestants did. As a result, many of us now feel at a loss when it comes to understanding—let alone explaining—the Bible to others. We fear the topic of the Bible coming up in conversation.

For many of us, the Bible was a very large book kept on a shelf in the living room or dining room and used mainly as a place to record the family history.

We feel intimidated by many of our Protestant brothers and sisters who can quote chapter and verse. Most of all, we have no idea what to tell someone if they should ask, "Is it *true* that Noah built an ark or that Adam lived to be 930 years old or that Jonah was swallowed by a large fish?" What do we say? How do we answer such questions? What do we believe for ourselves?

"I Was Never Taught to Read the Bible . . . "

For many of us, the Bible was a very large book kept on a shelf in the living room or dining room and used mainly as a place to record the family history. It was less a book to read than a relic to store in the house, a sacramental that reminded us of the presence of God's Word in the home. As children, many of us encountered the Bible only when we needed something heavy to flatten the wrinkles in a hastily glued school art project. Rare was the occasion that this great big book was pulled out to be read from. For one, it was too heavy. For another, it had words that sounded strange and foreign—too many "thee's" and "thou's" for our liking. More important, many of us were simply not encouraged to read the Bible. Some Catholics actually recall being discouraged from reading the Bible in the days before Vatican II.

Are You Biblically Deprived?

I grew up "biblically deprived." Don't get me wrong, I came from a good Catholic home. Like many Catholics of that time (the 1960s), our home had various Catholic sacramentals: a crucifix, small statues of the Sacred Heart of Jesus and the Blessed Virgin Mary, and a "God Bless Our Home" sign over the door. We also had a Bible. And like many good Catholics of the time, we never read it. No one told us to. It wasn't until years later that I took an interest in the Bible. When I give workshops to adults, I tell my story and then ask how many folks feel that they grew up "biblically deprived." Usually about 95 percent of the hands go up. The other 5 percent usually turn out to have been brought up in the Protestant Tradition!

Another reason Catholics shied away from the Bible was because we viewed the Bible as a Protestant thing. Suspicious of the axiom *Sola Scriptura!* (Scripture alone!), seen as a battle cry for Protestants, Catholics kept the Bible at arm's length, trusting the Church hierarchy, the nuns, and our CCD teachers to sort out the Bible messages intended for our ears. As long as we had the sacraments, Church Tradition, and Father's homily, we had little reason to sit down and read the Bible privately, let alone attempt to interpret the Word of God.

The Underlying Causes of Bibliaphobia

Most phobias are an exaggerated or irrational fear, dread, or aversion to any object or stimulus. In most cases, there may indeed be something to fear, but the fear becomes disproportional or irrational. Bibliaphobia works in much the same way. While it is true that there are some things about the Bible that may be intimidating, many of us avoid it as though it were a swarm of bees. Let's take a look at some of the more intimidating aspects of the Bible that may be at the root of our bibliaphobia.

> "The Bible tells us to love our neighbors and also to love our enemies; probably because they are generally the same people."
> —G.K. CHESTERTON

"It's too long!" Many of us may be accustomed to reading books that have legible print and are several hundred pages in length. The Bible, on the other hand, usually has very tiny print and contains anywhere between one thousand and two thousand five hundred pages, depending on which version we're reading.

"It has too many names I don't recognize." Eldad, Medad, Meshach, Shadrach, Abednego, Zephaniah, Zechariah, Caiaphas, Annas, etc. Who *are* these people? So-and-so begot so-and-so who begot so-and-so . . . These names don't ring any bells for us at first glance.

"It has too many places I've never heard of." Marah, Elim, Rephidim, Shiloh, Samaria, Colossae, Thessalonica—even the letter to the Philippians has nothing to do with the Philippines. Where *are* these places? It's hard to understand a story if we don't understand the setting.

"It uses images that don't belong to our time and culture." We live in an age of cell phones, the Internet, microwaves, CDs, DVDs, and HDTV. References to shekels, cubits, arks, wineskins, and mustard seeds often leave us scratching our heads.

"It's not like other books." Most books have a beginning, a middle, and an end and are divided up into chapters. The Bible has testaments, books, chapters, and verses. Most books that we read are chronological, however, the Bible seems to jump around a lot.

"Some of the stories just seem incredible." Most of us have never seen burning bushes, parting seas, arks, talking serpents, or people being swallowed by large fish. It's hard to understand these stories when we have no common frame of reference.

"You need to be a Scripture scholar to interpret the Bible." The Bible seems to be so complex and to contain so many layers of meaning that most of us feel inept and inadequate when it comes to making biblical interpretations. Sometimes it feels as if you need to study a whole semester of graduate theology just to understand a few passages.

"I don't know anything about Judaism and that's all the Old Testament talks about." Most of us are struggling just to be good Christians. The Bible, on the other hand—especially the Old Testament (which is three-quarters of the entire Bible)—seems to require a great deal of knowledge about the Jewish faith and way of life.

"I honestly don't know if I can stomach some of it." Jesus talks about loving enemies, praying for persecutors, turning the other cheek, the blessings of being poor, and dying in order to live. How do we live these ideas today? Can we?

"I could never quote chapter and verse like many Protestants can!" On TV and in life, we see so many preachers, ministers, and ordinary people—most often Protestant—who can quote the Bible from memory, citing chapter and verse. Do we need to learn the Bible that way, too? Many of us are not sure if we can or even want to.

Perhaps noting all of these common fears and concerns about the Bible has only confirmed your notion that the Bible is something to shy away from. On the contrary, I am just pointing out that these fears and concerns about the Bible are not yours alone. They are shared by many people, especially Catholics who have not had much Bible exposure and experience. But do not despair! Fear of the Bible can be overcome by tackling the above-mentioned concerns with a commonsense understanding of the Bible, such as how it is put together and how we are to read and interpret it.

So, how can you tell if you are suffering from bibliaphobia? Take the following quiz.

"'The last shall be first, and the first last.' I assume there was some sort of slip-up in the copying room."

Determine your level of bibliaphobic behavior by using the scale below to respond to each of the symptoms in this checklist.

0 = Totally Disagree **2** = Somewhat Agree
1 = Somewhat Disagree **3** = Totally Agree

_____ You have trouble locating even famous Bible stories and characters.

_____ You shy away from discussions about the Bible.

_____ You feel intimidated by those who you feel have more Bible knowledge than yourself.

_____ You have difficulty answering questions that children ask you about the Bible.

_____ You rarely attempt reading the Bible on your own.

_____ You feel inadequate when you consider attending Bible study.

_____ Locating a passage identified by book, chapter, and verse (e.g., 1 Pt 2:3) seems as difficult as solving an algebra problem.

_____ After reading a Bible passage, you often feel you have no idea what it meant.

_____ You find many Bible stories confusing.

_____ Your Bible is still in store-bought "mint" condition. (Give yourself an extra point if it is still encased in the store's shrink-wrap.)

_____ **Write your total here.**

Now, match your score to one of these categories.

0 = **None:** You're perfectly at home with the Bible.
1–10 = **Mild:** The Bible presents some challenges to you.
11–20 = **Moderate:** You find the Bible to be most difficult.
21–29 = **Severe:** You have a strong fear of the Bible.
30–31 = **Bibliaphobe Alert:** You need immediate Bible therapy!

Acknowledging the Problem

Our lack of knowledge about the Bible can often be an embarrassment. How can we, adult Catholic Christians, admit to not knowing or understanding the Word of God? We may not even realize how inadequate our understanding of the Bible really is until we are put to the test.

Did someone suggest a test? Take the following quiz to see just how familiar (or unfamiliar) you are with the Bible and its contents.

Quiz

Time yourself as you find each of these stories or passages in the Bible. Write down how long it takes you to find each one. If you are able to find a story or passage in two minutes or fewer, place a check mark next to it.

_____ David and Goliath

_____ Noah's ark

_____ Jonah and the large fish

_____ Moses crossing the Red Sea

_____ Daniel in the lion's den

_____ Zacchaeus the tax collector

_____ Jesus walking on the water

_____ Pentecost

_____ Hg 2:1–3

_____ The second book of Chronicles, chapter 29, verses 9–15

Now, match the number of check marks to one of the categories below to determine your BQ (Bible Quotient).

> 10 = **High:** You probably don't need to read the rest of *The Bible Blueprint*.
> 7–9 = **Average:** Not bad, but keep reading.
> 3–6 = **Fair:** *The Bible Blueprint* is required reading.
> 0–2 = **Low:** You *need The Bible Blueprint*.

This very unscientific test is only an indicator of how familiar or unfamiliar you are with the Bible. However, the reason we are not familiar with the Bible is because we often do not understand it, and as a result, we fear it. We always tend to fear those things with which we are most unfamiliar. We need to overcome our fears of the Bible by becoming more familiar with the Good Book. Don't let bibliaphobia get the best of you. Don't become an adult "Charlie Brown"—paralyzed by a fear that prevents you from living fully by discovering in the Bible what it truly means to live!

Four brothers left home for college and they each became financially well off. Some years later, they discussed the gifts they were able to give their elderly mother who lived far away in another city. The first brother said, "I had a big house built for Mamma." The second said, "I had a hundred-thousand-dollar theater built in the house." The third said, "I had my Mercedes dealer deliver an SL600 to her." Finally, the fourth said, "You know how Mamma loved reading the Bible and you know she can't read anymore because she can't see very well. I spent one hundred thousand dollars on a parrot that can recite the entire Bible. Mamma just has to name the chapter and verse and the parrot will recite it." The other brothers were impressed. After the holidays, Mom sent out her thank-you notes. She wrote: "Milton, the house you built is so huge I live in only one room, but I have to clean the whole house. Thanks anyway." "Michael, the home theater could hold fifty people, but all of my friends are dead, I've lost my hearing, and I'm nearly blind. I'll never use it. Thank you for the gesture, just the same." "Marvin, I am too old to travel. I stay home and I have my groceries delivered, so I never use the Mercedes. The thought was good. Thanks." "Dearest Melvin, you were the only son to have the good sense to give a little thought to your gift. The chicken was delicious. Thank you!"

And Now, the Good News

The good news (aside from the gospel of Jesus Christ) is that, with a few tips and some practice, reading and understanding the Bible can become much easier and extremely fulfilling. The Bible was not written for scholars, it was written for you and me. The Bible is God speaking to you and me in the course of human events. It is meant to be read not only in churches and universities, but also in subways, at bus stops, in the cafeteria, in a rocking chair, or in bed, or listened to on CD or podcast as you drive. Sure, certain aspects of the Bible may seem intimidating, but when you stop to think about the fact that the Creator of the universe has something to say to *you,* it makes the notion of learning about the Bible a little bit more enticing!

The Bible has been a powerful influence in my life and in the lives of countless numbers of people. Not only is it the story of people who lived thousands of years ago, but it is also the story of your life and my life. Every Bible story is a metaphor for the many experiences of God we all have had and will have in our lives. So, as we prepare to look at burning bushes, parting seas, the calming of storms, the raisings from the dead, and the healing of blind, deaf, and paralyzed people, know that somehow these experiences are part of our story.

Overcoming bibliaphobia is a matter of changing our perception of the Bible. The first thing we need to realize when considering the Good Book is that it isn't a book at all! The word *biblia* comes from the Greek, meaning "books." In reality, the Bible is a *collection* of books—seventy-three in all. For that reason, I prefer to think of the Bible as God's Library. What is a library other

The Bible was not written for scholars, it was written for you and me.

than books brought together in one place in order to give readers access to the entire collection? When we understand the Bible as God's Library, it changes our approach to how we are to read and understand its writings. We would never go to a library and read the first book on the first shelf, and then the second book on the first shelf, and keep on going until we have read the last book on the last shelf. Nor would we suppose that all of the books in a library are to be understood and read in exactly the same way or that all are the same type of literature. Once we learn how to use a library, we are capable of accessing the power of its collection. In the same way, once we learn how to use God's Library, the Bible, we will be able to access the mighty power of its contents.

So, welcome to God's Library. Leave your bibliaphobia at the door and enter into a collection of writings about how God powerfully lives and moves in the lives of some very interesting people—including *you.*

Questions for Reflection and Discussion

- What was your experience of the Bible as a child? a teen? a young adult? What is your experience presently?

- What do you find most intimidating about the Bible?

- What do you find most attractive or inviting about the Bible?

- Which of your friends or acquaintances knows the Bible extremely well? Where did he or she get their knowledge of the Bible?

- How might a better understanding of the Bible make a difference in your life?

- When it comes to reading the Bible, what is the biggest obstacle you would like to overcome?

- How have you used libraries? Think about how libraries work and keep this understanding handy as you continue to read this book and become more familiar with God's Library, the Bible.

Chapter Three

Preparing to Enter God's Library

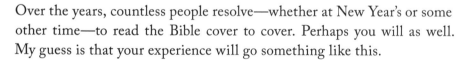

It's common to use the word *blueprint* when referring to any kind of a plan. We speak of a blueprint for success, a blueprint for the nation's economy, and a blueprint for world peace. Basically, we use the word blueprint to describe the existence of a plan. As we approach the Bible, it's good to know that there is a plan to how the Bible is put together. The Bible—God's library—has a blueprint that, if followed, can make it easy for you and me to "walk through it" without getting lost.

Over the years, countless people resolve—whether at New Year's or some other time—to read the Bible cover to cover. Perhaps you will as well. My guess is that your experience will go something like this.

You begin with a great deal of enthusiasm, perhaps parceling out a special time each day to devote to reading the Bible.

Genesis has enough interesting stories to keep you going but gives rather too much practical advice on ark building.

Most of Exodus is full of drama, with the ten plagues and the Red Sea, and rebuilds the enthusiasm that began to flag in the genealogy sections of Genesis.

This sacred tradition, therefore, and Sacred Scripture of both the Old and New Testaments are like a mirror in which the pilgrim Church on earth looks at God, from whom she has received everything, until she is brought finally to see Him as He is, face to face (see 1 John 3:2). (*Dei Verbum*, 7)

Leviticus is often the deal breaker. Laws, rules, directions, and penalties—ugh! And if you somehow manage to make it through Leviticus, Numbers is almost guaranteed to finish you off.

You give up on your reading project, concluding that the Bible is a book written for scholars and not for ordinary folks like us.

Why do I make this dire prediction? Simply because reading the Bible from cover to cover is a flawed approach that treats the Bible like an ordinary book. Even such humongous tomes as *War and Peace* can be conquered using this basic head-down, barrel-through method of reading cover to cover. However, the Bible is no ordinary book. It is a collection of books, a library. Sure, the Bible *can* be read from cover to cover, and many have done so with great delight. However, many others have tried and failed, only to miss out on the powerful message of God's Word. We need to approach the Bible as if we were exploring the blueprints of a library building. Like any library, the Bible is divided into a number of sections, making available to us a rich variety of readings from which we may choose according to our needs and tastes. Consider the Bible a library that you will become more familiar with over time. A quick study of the blueprints for God's library will help you to become more familiar with how the Bible is arranged. The more familiar you become with God's Library, the more you will use it. The more you use it, the more of it you will read and understand. The more of it you read and understand, the closer you will be to the God who speaks to you in and through it.

"The length of each board was ten cubits, and the breadth of a board one cubit and a half. One board had two tenons, equally distant one from another: thus did he make for all the boards of the tabernacle. And he made boards for the tabernacle; twenty boards for the south side southward: and forty sockets of silver he made under the twenty boards; two sockets under one board for his two tenons, and two sockets under another board for his two tenons. And for th..."

"The Reading through the Bible Hour" began to run into ratings problems in Exodus 36.

How a Library Works

Let's flesh out this comparison between the Bible and a library by thinking about how we use our local libraries and how we might "use" the Bible. Over the course of our lives, most of us have made numerous trips to libraries in our schools and communities. We go for various reasons: research, enrichment, entertainment, to find peace and quiet, etc. But once we're there, how do we use a library? It's easy. For most of us, it entails the following:

> **Consider the Bible a library that you will become more familiar with over time. The more familiar you become with God's Library, the more you will use it.**

- check the online card catalog for the location of a particular author or book title or a type of subject matter, or ask a librarian to point out the location of a particular type of literature

- locate the section of the library in which that type of literature (or in which the book's assigned number) can be found

- locate the item(s) you are interested in reading

- check out the item(s)

- take the item(s) home and read at your leisure or as needed

Libraries are familiar, often comforting, places. Unless you were shushed one too many times as a child, we tend not to associate anxiety with visiting the library. So, with that in mind, let's visit God's Library. We come to God's Library for many reasons: research, prayer, inspiration, curiosity, enjoyment, encouragement, etc. We also come to it with different tastes. Some of us prefer the psalms and the proverbs to the letters and the parables.

Let's take a closer look now at the various parts of God's library.

Using the Catalog

Nowadays, nearly all library card catalogs are computerized. However, the basic idea has not changed. You can still locate a book using the author's name or the book's title, or you can use a keyword search to find books on a particular subject (more on this later). Many of us, when looking for a particular book, are guilty of ignoring the catalog at the library and heading straight for the shelves. More often than not, we end up searching aisle after aisle and shelf after shelf with little or no luck. In much the same way, many of us attempt to locate particular Scripture passages in the Bible without using the "catalog," or the table of contents. If we know the book, chapter, and verses that we are looking for, the Bible's table of contents will help us. Later, we'll learn how to find a Bible passage when we don't know its book, chapter, or verse. In a Bible's table of contents, you will more than likely find the following:

- a list of the books of the Bible in the order in which they appear in the Old and New Testaments, as well as the page number on which each book begins

- an alphabetical listing of the books

- an alphabetical listing of the abbreviation of each book

A table of contents page in a typical Bible will look something like this.

Old Testament

Book	Abbreviation	Page
Genesis	Gn	1
Exodus	Ex	50
Leviticus	Lv	100
Numbers	Nm	130
Deuteronomy	Dt	170

. . . and so on, listing all forty-six Old Testament books. In the same way, the New Testament listing will look like this.

New Testament

Book	Abbreviation	Page
Matthew	Mt	1000
Mark	Mk	1050
Luke	Lk	1075
John	Jn	1115

. . . and so on, listing all twenty-seven New Testament books. (Some Bibles start over at page 1 for the New Testament.) For a complete list of all of the books of the Bible and their abbreviations, see page 118 of the Bible Resources section of this book (or pick up a Bible and check it out for yourself).

Sometimes a table of contents will include a separate alphabetical listing of the books in the Old and New Testaments. It might look something like this.

Old Testament

Book	Abbreviation	Page
Amos	Am	900
Baruch	Bar	.875
1 Chronicles	1 Chr	350
2 Chronicles	2 Chr	400
Daniel	Dn	950

. . . and so on.

New Testament

Book	Abbreviation	Page
Acts of the Apostles	Acts	1200
Colossians	Col	1300
1 Corinthians	1 Cor	1250
2 Corinthians	2 Cor	1275
Ephesians	Eph	1290

. . . and so on.

Now that we see how the Bible's catalog is arranged, let's take a closer look at how to use it.

Is It "Judg.," "Jg," or "Jgs"?

Learning to use the abbreviation page of your Bible is critical to being able to locate Bible passages. One thing to consider, however, is that not all Bibles abbreviate books in the same way. A little later on, we'll discuss the differences between various Bibles and how to choose one, but for now, just know that different Bibles abbreviate the names of books in different ways. For example, the book of Judges can be found abbreviated as Judg., Jg, or Jgs, depending on which Bible translation you are looking at. Knowing that Bibles abbreviate books differently will help avoid a great deal of confusion, especially if you are in a group of people using a variety of Bible translations or editions.

The Bible's Book Numbering System

In any library, you need to understand the numbering system used to shelve the books in a particular order so that you can find what you need. The same is true of locating passages in God's Library. No, the Bible uses neither Dewey decimal classification nor the Library of Congress classification system, but instead has its own system of identifying books, chapters, and verses. It's called Scripture citation. You've seen it before. It looks like this.

> 1 Pt 2:1–4

And like any system of classification, it will look like a foreign language until you learn the rules. The key to understanding Scripture citation is really quite simple. No matter the Bible translation or edition you are using, citations always follow this format: the name of the book, followed by the chapter number, followed by the verse number (or the beginning and ending verse numbers).

> "It is good to read the testimonies of Scripture;
> it is good to seek the Lord our God in them."
> —SAINT FRANCIS OF ASSISI

The chapter number and the verse number(s) are separated by a colon. So,

1 Pt 2:1–4

means

1 Pt (name of the book) 2 (chapter number):1–4 (verses 1 through 4)

But what's a 1 Pt? If you refer to the abbreviation section in the alphabetical listing of books in your Bible's table of contents, you'll discover that 1 Pt is the First Letter of Peter. So, the citation refers to the First Letter of Peter, chapter 2, verses 1 through 4.

Here are a few more examples.

Jgs 15:6–15 = the book of Judges, chapter 15, verses 6 through 15

Zep 3:18–19 = the book of Zephaniah, chapter 3, verses 18 through 19

Jn 7:3–6, 10 = the Gospel of John, chapter 7, verses 3 through 6 and verse 10

Ti 2:11–14 = the Letter to Titus, chapter 2, verses 11 through 14

A man's business is going down the drain. He is very depressed and doesn't know what to do. He goes to the priest who tells him, "Take a beach chair and a Bible and put them in your car and drive down to the edge of the ocean. Go to the water's edge. Take the beach chair out of the car, sit on it, and take the Bible out and open it up. The wind will riffle the pages for a while and eventually the Bible will stay open at a particular page. Read the first words your eyes fall on and they will tell you what to do." The man does as he is told. He sits on the chair at the water's edge and opens the Bible. The wind riffles the pages of the Bible and then stops at a particular page. He looks down at the Bible and his eyes fall on words, which tell him what he has to do. Three months later, the man, wearing a thousand-dollar Italian suit, comes back to see the priest and hands him a thick envelope full of money, telling him that he wants to donate this money to the parish in order to thank the priest for his wonderful advice. The priest is delighted. He asks him what words in the Bible brought this good fortune to him. The man replies, "Chapter 11."

Quiz 1

Practice with the following Scripture citations. If you need help with the abbreviations, use your Bible's table of contents or see page 118 of this book. The answers can be found at the bottom of the page.

1. Is 42:5–10 _____

2. Hg 2:6–11 _____

3. 1 Mc 6:1–6 _____

4. 3 Jn 1:2–4 _____

5. Jas 2:7–9 _____

6. Mk 9:8–15 _____

Quiz 2

Now, try the same thing but in reverse order: take the following passages described in prose and write them in citation form. The first one has been done as an example. The answers can be found at the bottom of the page.

1. The book of Daniel, chapter 4, verse 11 _____ Dn 4:11 _____

2. The Letter to the Romans, chapter 5, verses 3 to 6 _____

3. The book of Judith, chapter 2, verses 9 to 16 _____

4. The book of Habakkuk, chapter 3, verse 12 _____

5. The Gospel of Matthew, chapter 5, verses 1 to 9 _____

Quiz 1 Answers

1. The book of Isaiah, chapter 42, verses 5–10; **2.** The book of Haggai, chapter 2, verses 6–11; **3.** The First book of Maccabees, chapter 6, verses 1–6; **4.** The Third Letter of John, chapter 1, verses 2–4; **5.** The Letter of James, chapter 2, verses 7–9; **6.** The Gospel of Mark, chapter 9, verses 8–15.

Quiz 2 Answers

2. Rom 5:3–6; **3.** Jdt 2:9–16; **4.** Hb 3:12; **5.** Mt 5:1–9.

Now that you know how to locate passages by book, chapter, and verse, let's turn to how you can locate a particular story in the Bible when you have no idea what book it is in.

Questions for Reflection and Discussion

- Have you ever tried reading the Bible cover to cover? If so, what was that experience like?

- What parts of the Bible have you read? What parts do you find most enjoyable? What parts do you find most difficult to read?

- How familiar are you with the use of Scripture citation? How skilled are you at finding a Bible passage when given a Scripture citation?

- Look through your Bible's table of contents. What features do you find most helpful? What features are you not finding there (for example, a list of abbreviations of the books of the Bible) that you may need to locate elsewhere?

- In what ways can the table of contents pages of your Bible be of assistance to you in your prayer life? in your Bible study?

Mathematician Bert Mewhausen spends his spare time looking for scriptural solutions to life's problems.

Chapter Four

The Bible's Floor Plan

One of the first things included in a blueprint is the basement floor plan which shows the location of the walls that will support the entire structure. As we look at the blueprint for God's library—the Bible—a good place for us to start is with the floor plan so that we can come to recognize the foundation upon which the structure of the Bible rests.

Think back to when you learned how to ride a two-wheeler. More than likely, you used training wheels until you developed your own sense of balance. After much practice, the training wheels came off and you were on your way. In the same way, we are going to look at a simple tool that can be used like training wheels until you develop your own sense of how to maneuver through the Bible.

What should you do when you want to find the story of David and Goliath but you don't know what book it is in? How does one develop a familiarity with the Bible so that wonderful stories and famous characters can be quickly located? In the back of this book you will find eight bookmarks (pages 125–131). You may cut these out or copy the text onto heavy stock to use as bookmarks.

A quick look at the floor plan of God's library—the Bible—reveals to us that the Bible is split into two main sections, the Old and New Testaments. Both the Old and New Testaments are then divided again into four more sections. These divisions are listed in the table on the next page.

And here, in order to strengthen Our teaching and Our exhortations, it is well to recall how, from the beginning of Christianity, all who have been renowned for holiness of life and sacred learning have given their deep and constant attention to Holy Scripture. (*Providentissimus Deus*, 7)

Old Testament	New Testament
Pentateuch (Torah)	Gospels
History	Acts
Wisdom	Letters
Prophets	Revelation

Now that we know the names, let's do a little exercise. Using your Bible's table of contents, locate the last page of the book of Malachi (which is the last page of the Old Testament) and the first page of the Gospel of Matthew (which is the first page of the New Testament). Now, take a look at how the Bible is separated. Observe how large the Old Testament is compared to the New Testament. Now, consider the clearest and most simple distinction between the Old and New Testaments.

Is this story directly related to the life of Jesus and the early Church? If the answer is yes, then you'll be looking in the New Testament. If not, you'll be searching through the Old Testament.

The Old Testament is the story of God's relationship with the people of Israel *before* the birth of Jesus Christ.

The New Testament is the story of God's relationship with the People of God beginning with the life, death, Resurrection, and ascension of Jesus Christ and continuing with the early Church.

Once you have this clear distinction in your head, you will have a better understanding of where to begin searching for stories in the Bible by asking yourself one simple question: is this story directly related to the life of Jesus and the early Church? If the answer is yes, then you'll be looking in the New Testament. If not, you'll be searching through the Old Testament.

"Great," you may be saying, "but I still have to sift through a thousand pages to find the story I'm looking for!" This is true, but what we are about to do is to break the Bible down into the smaller sections mentioned in the table. The following outlines, which are also found on the bookmarks, can be seen as a brief introduction to the highlights of each section of the Bible. By using the bookmarks and the highlights outline, you can have easy access to the various parts of the Bible.

Highlights of the Old Testament

Find the four bookmarks for the Old Testament that you cut out of the back of this book (see page 125) or that you copied onto another sheet of paper. Lay them out side by side next to your Bible.

Pentateuch: The first five books of the Old Testament, Genesis through Deuteronomy Place the Pentateuch (pronounced `Pen-tuh-took) bookmark on the last page of the book of Deuteronomy. The pages from the beginning of Genesis to this bookmark make up the section called Pentateuch (Torah in the Hebrew Scriptures), meaning the five books of the Law. This section captures the beginnings of the relationship between God and the people of Israel with the central focus being the Exodus event—the experience of being led from slavery to freedom. Here are some of the highlights of this section:

- the Creation stories
- Adam and Eve
- Cain and Abel
- Noah's ark
- the Tower of Babel
- Sodom and Gomorrah
- Abraham and Sarah
- Isaac and Rebekah
- Jacob and Esau
- Joseph (the coat of many colors)

"Okay, four-year-olds! Let's polish off the book of Leviticus!"

- Moses (in the reeds, the burning bush, the ten plagues, the crossing of the Red Sea, the Passover, the Ten Commandments, the Ark of the Covenant, the journey through the desert, the death of Moses)
- the twelve tribes of Israel
- the laws, traditions, and feasts of Israel

Why Did the NAB Do That?

The prefix *penta* means "five." The *Pentateuch*, of course, consists of five books: Genesis, Exodus, Leviticus, Numbers, and Deuteronomy. Don't be confused, then, if you have a New American Bible in which you'll find that the table of contents lists eight books in the Pentateuch: Genesis through Deuteronomy as well as Joshua, Judges, and Ruth.

"Why's that?" you may ask. Basically, the editors of the NAB made this decision based on the fact that many early Greek manuscripts united Joshua, Judges, and Ruth with the Pentateuch because of the similarity in style and origin they all possess. The book of Joshua completes the Exodus narrative in that it demonstrates how God remained faithful in his promise of giving to the Israelites the land he had promised. Thus, the book of Joshua, together with the Pentateuch comprises what is known as the *Hexateuch*.

But wait, there's more! The book of Judges contains an introduction (chapters 1–3) that connects it with the Joshua narrative, describing the events that followed the death of Joshua. Finally, until the fifth century, the book of Ruth was viewed as a part of the book of Judges. It is because of these connections that the books of Joshua, Judges, and Ruth are seen as related to or connected with the Pentateuch, although not technically a part of it. In fact, these eight books are sometimes referred to as the *Octateuch*. No kidding!

History: Joshua through 2 Maccabees Place the bookmark labeled History on the last page of 2 Maccabees. The section from the Pentateuch bookmark to this bookmark makes up the History section of the Bible. This section records the story of the people of Israel who, under various leaders (judges and kings), fought to establish and keep the Promised Land. Here are the highlights of this section:

- Joshua (crossing the Jordan, the walls of Jericho)
- Samson and Delilah
- Ruth and Naomi
- Samuel (request for a king)
- King Saul

- David and Goliath; King David

- Solomon (the temple, Queen of Sheba)

- Elijah and Elisha

- many kings, battles, and genealogies

- division of the kingdom

- Exile and return

- Judith and Esther

Wisdom: Job through Sirach Place the bookmark labeled Wisdom at the end of the book of Sirach (or Ecclesiasticus, as it is called in some Bibles). You're now ready to explore the Wisdom section of the Bible, which includes everything from the History bookmark to this bookmark. While the Bible is full of wisdom, this particular section gathers together all the wisdom teachings of the people of Israel that were collected over thousands of years of wandering the desert, living in the Promised Land, worshiping in the temple, and struggling through the Exile. This section includes many anecdotes, sayings, prayers, poems, and songs. Here are some highlights:

- Job's suffering

- 150 Psalms for all occasions

- hundreds of proverbs

- wise sayings, including "Vanity of vanities! All things are vanity!" and "There is a time for everything" and "A faithful friend is a sturdy shelter"

- a romantic love song (Song of Songs, or Song of Solomon)

- thousands more sayings about wisdom, prudence, good health, wealth, holiness, family, friends, misery, death, and even table etiquette

Are the Psalms Wisdom Literature?

While the Psalms are not technically considered wisdom literature (they are more appropriately liturgical hymns), Psalms traditionally have been placed with the Wisdom books.

Prophets: Isaiah through Malachi Place the last of your four Old Testament bookmarks, labeled Prophets, at the end of the book of Malachi, which is also the last page of the Old Testament. Welcome to the last section of the Old Testament—the Prophets (everything from your Wisdom bookmark to this one). The prophets were not concerned with foretelling the future. Their purpose was to call the people of Israel to return to their past fidelity to God lest they face dire consequences. And when the people of Israel found themselves mired in the Exile, the prophets held out hope for the future. This hope was the promise of a messiah and an everlasting kingdom. Yet, even these assurances of a future are accompanied by a call for a return to the fidelity of the past. Here are some highlights:

- The major (meaning lengthier) prophets
  - Isaiah (Immanuel, "the people who walked in darkness have seen a great light," "comfort my people," etc.)
  - Jeremiah (call of Jeremiah, Exile and return)
  - Ezekiel (the dry bones)
- The minor (meaning briefer) prophets
  - Daniel (the lion's den, Shadrach, Meshach, and Abednego)
  - Hosea (the unfaithful wife)
  - Joel (the Day of the Lord)
  - Amos (the call to justice)
  - Jonah (swallowed by a large fish)

"Your furnace is pretty outdated I can see the footprints of Shadrach, Meshach, and Abed-nego."

Highlights of the New Testament

Find the four bookmarks for the New Testament that you cut out of the back of this book (see page 129) or that you copied onto another sheet of paper. Lay them out side by side next to your Bible.

Gospels: Matthew, Mark, Luke, and John Place the bookmark labeled Gospels at the end of the Gospel of John. Between the bookmark for the Prophets and this bookmark is the beginning of the New Testament. It is also the section of the Bible in which we walk with Jesus. The Gospels (Matthew, Mark, Luke, and John) contain the stories that are most sacred to our Christian faith and heritage: stories of the life, teachings, miracles, Passion, death, and Resurrection of Jesus of Nazareth. If you're looking for a story about Jesus, this is the place to look. Here are some highlights:

The Gospels (Matthew, Mark, Luke, and John) contain the stories that are most sacred to our Christian faith and heritage: stories of the life, teachings, miracles, Passion, death, and Resurrection of Jesus of Nazareth.

- the birth of Jesus (the Magi, the shepherds, etc.)

- the Holy Family (Mary and Joseph)

- the finding of Jesus in the temple

- the temptation in the desert and the baptism of Jesus

- the Beatitudes and the Our Father

- parables (the prodigal son, the Good Samaritan, the sower, the mustard seed, etc.)

- the Golden Rule and the Great Commandment

- numerous miracles (calming of the storm, raising of Lazarus, changing water into wine, feeding of the five thousand, walking on water, healing of the blind, deaf, and paralyzed, etc.)

- the Last Supper, Eucharist, and the washing of the feet

- the Agony in the Garden

- Peter's denial and Judas's betrayal

- the way of the cross

- the Crucifixion

- the Resurrection and appearances
- dozens of fascinating characters: Zacchaeus, Pontius Pilate, Mary Magdalene, Nicodemus, the Samaritan woman, Martha and Mary, etc.
- powerful images such as the Bread of Life, the Light of the World, and the Way, the Truth, and the Life

Who Wrote the Gospels?

We sometimes think that the Gospels were written as the events took place, as though the Evangelists were reporters "on the scene." Or, we may think that a few short years after the events took place, each of the Evangelists was seized by a moment of inspiration, picked up a plume, and transcribed their Gospels as dictated by the Holy Spirit. Actually, the Gospels were proclaimed orally for decades before they were gathered into written form.

- Mark's Gospel was written first, shortly before the year AD 70.
- The Gospels of Matthew and Luke (both using Mark's Gospel as a resource) were written shortly after AD 70.
- Finally, the Gospel of John was written about twenty years after Matthew and Luke.

It is not likely that the Evangelists (Matthew, Mark, Luke, and John) actually put pen to paper. They were most likely deceased by the time their accounts were recorded in written form by loyal followers. When we say that the Gospels were inspired, we are saying that this entire process was guided by the Holy Spirit.

Acts of the Apostles Getting to know this section of the Bible is easy because it is just one book: the Acts of the Apostles. Place the bookmark labeled Acts of the Apostles at the end of this book and relive the experience of the early Christian community. In many ways, the book of Acts is a sequel to the Gospel of Luke because Luke and Acts were written by the same author. Here are some highlights of the Acts:

- Jesus' ascension
- the descent of the Holy Spirit at Pentecost

- descriptions of the communal life of the early Church

- Stephen's martyrdom

- Philip and the Ethiopian

- Saul's conversion and baptism

- the missionary work of Peter, Saul (Paul), Barnabas, and others

- miracles performed through Peter and Paul

- Paul's travels, imprisonment, trials, shipwreck, and arrival in Rome

Letters (also called Epistles): Romans through Jude Place the bookmark labeled Letters at the end of the Letter of Jude. Everything from the Acts of the Apostles bookmark up to this one represents the communications of the early Church, before e-mails, phones, and faxes. A little more than half of the twenty-one letters, or epistles, are attributed to Paul and the Pauline tradition. All of the letters are addressed to communities of Christians and to the leaders of these communities, and were designed to teach, admonish, encourage, correct, and update the various churches. Here are some highlights:

- The letters of Paul (such as Romans, 1 and 2 Corinthians, Galatians, and Ephesians) feature theology, teachings, and exhortations concerning
  - grace
  - justification by faith
  - the Law
  - the Eucharist
  - the metaphor of the Body
  - variety and unity of gifts
  - ministry
  - suffering
  - Christ and his cross
  - Christian conduct

PAUL HEARS FROM HIS MOTHER

You have time to write to the Corinthians and the Galatians, but never to me...

Copyright © Doug Hall, 1991. Used by Permission.

- James (faith and good works, Anointing of the Sick)

- 1 Peter (be prepared to explain your hope)

- 1 John ("Beloved, let us love one another . . .")

Revelation Place the last bookmark, labeled Revelation, at the end of the book of Revelation and you've reached the end of the Bible. As you enter the book of Revelation, be aware that it is one of the most misunderstood books of the Bible. Many falsely use this book to predict the end of the world. Written in apocalyptic style, the book of Revelation uses many symbols and figurative language to describe the eternal struggle between good and evil. Despite all of the frightening imagery, the uplifting conclusion of this book is that good has and always will prevail. Here are the highlights:

> **As you enter the book of Revelation, be aware that it is one of the most misunderstood books of the Bible.**

- visions and messages to the seven churches
- the scroll and the lamb
- the one hundred forty-four thousand saved
- the seven trumpets
- the woman and the dragon
- the King of kings
- the thousand-year reign
- the new heavens and new earth
- the new Jerusalem
- "Come, Lord Jesus!"

> "There's nothing written in the Bible, Old or New Testament, that says, 'If you believe in Me, you ain't going to have no troubles.'"
> —RAY CHARLES

Practicing with Your "Training Wheels"

Now that your bookmarks are in place, practice locating some of the highlights outlined on the bookmarks themselves or on the previous few pages. Browse through a section of the Bible and search for some of the famous characters and place names. Don't set out to read whole sections. For now, just browse around until you discover passages that you are particularly interested in reading right now. If you don't understand a section or the reading is becoming tedious and difficult to understand, move on.

As you become more and more skilled at Bible reading, you can return to the more difficult and challenging sections. As you tackle these more difficult sections, you may wish to consult books about the Bible that can help you make sense of what you are reading. (See page 114 for a list of suggested readings.) For now, focus on getting to know the sections of the Bible so that you've got a firm sense of what can be found in each section. Most important, use your bookmarks to become more familiar with where these various sections of the Bible are. Your bookmarks will act as training wheels for the time being, assisting you in traversing the terrain of the Bible. Eventually, however, the training wheels must come off. When you feel you have worked hard at getting to know the locations of the various sections of the Bible, remove your bookmarks and continue trying to locate passages, stories, and characters in their respective sections. You should find that by familiarizing yourself with the themes and topics treated in various sections, you are able to find particular stories and passages more quickly and with greater confidence.

Develop your Bible blueprint skills by doing the following exercise.

> A catechist asked his class to draw pictures of their favorite Bible stories. He was puzzled by Sandy's picture, which showed four people on an airplane, so he asked her which story it was meant to represent. "The flight to Egypt," said Sandy. "I see . . . and that must be Mary, Joseph, and Baby Jesus," the catechist said. "But who's the fourth person?" "Oh, that's Pontius," replied Sandy, "the Pilot."

Read the list of stories and characters below and match the letter of the section of the Bible that you believe includes this story or character. The answers can be found at the bottom of the page.

a. Pentateuch   **c.** Wisdom   **e.** Gospels   **g.** Letters
b. History   **d.** Prophets   **f.** Acts   **h.** Revelation

_____ **1.** Solomon's Temple

_____ **2.** The seventh trumpet

_____ **3.** Jonah and the large fish

_____ **4.** Saul's conversion

_____ **5.** Noah's ark

_____ **6.** Jacob and Esau

_____ **7.** The scriptural way of the cross

_____ **8.** Stephen's martyrdom

_____ **9.** Paul writing to the people of Ephesus

_____ **10.** The New Jerusalem

_____ **11.** David and Goliath

_____ **12.** Moses and the burning bush

_____ **13.** Zacchaeus

_____ **14.** The raising of Lazarus

_____ **15.** The dry bones

_____ **16.** Joseph, "the coat of many colors"

_____ **17.** Justification by faith

_____ **18.** The Holy Spirit at Pentecost

_____ **19.** Samson and Delilah

_____ **20.** The Ten Commandments

Quiz Answers
1. b; 2. h; 3. d; 4. f; 5. a; 6. a; 7. e; 8. f; 9. g; 10. h;
11. b; 12. a; 13. e; 14. e; 15. d; 16. a; 17. g; 18. f; 19. b; 20. a.

Questions for Reflection and Discussion

- Which Bible stories are the most difficult for you to find?

- What are the eight sections of God's library? Can you briefly summarize what and who can be found in each (without peeking at the bookmarks)?

- How can dividing the Bible into these eight sections help you in your knowledge of and familiarity with the Bible?

- As you practiced with your bookmarks, which section of the Bible did you discover for the first time?

- What section of the Bible do you look forward to getting to know better? Why?

Chapter Five

Information Blocks:
Footnotes and Cross-References

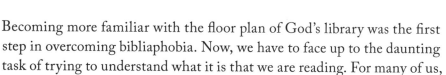

Blueprints do not consist solely of drawings. Any construction worker or craftsman will tell you that, in addition to the sketches, there are information blocks that provide additional explanation about specifications, materials, and other details that the sketches alone do not provide. When it comes to reading and interpreting the Bible, we too need additional information.

Becoming more familiar with the floor plan of God's library was the first step in overcoming bibliaphobia. Now, we have to face up to the daunting task of trying to understand what it is that we are reading. For many of us, once we actually find the Scripture passage, our joy is short-lived because we realize that we are dealing with material that was written long ago in a land far away from our front door. We get frustrated when we realize that we have little or no idea of what it is that we are reading or how to properly understand it. We need some assistance in accessing and unleashing the power of God's Word.

For the correct understanding of what the sacred author wanted to assert, due attention must be paid to the customary and characteristic styles of feeling, speaking and narrating which prevailed at the time of the sacred writer, and to the patterns men normally employed at that period in their everyday dealings with one another. (*Dei Verbum*, 12)

So far, we've been talking about the blueprints or floor plan for God's library, the Bible. Let's turn our attention now to another helpful metaphor for the Bible—a time capsule.

We all know what a time capsule is and how it works. People gather objects that convey the experience of their time—the fads, the defining moments, the customs, the famous people, the music, the headlines, the milestones, the accomplishments, and so on. These objects are placed in a container that is sealed and buried or placed somewhere with the idea that it will not be unearthed or opened until a much later date by people of another time, another era, or another experience.

We need some assistance in accessing and unleashing the power of God's Word.

The hope is that when people of some future era uncover the time capsule and examine the objects placed within, the experience of the past will come alive for them. By examining these objects from the past and seeking explanations for items that are foreign and mysterious, the people who unearthed the time capsule will make a connection with the people who buried it years before. The Bible attempts to do the very same thing for us. In many ways, the Bible is also a time capsule from the people of Israel and the early Church.

My, How Things Have Changed!

Change used to occur very slowly in our world—until the Industrial Revolution, that is. Cultures and societies that remained virtually unchanged for centuries suddenly faced an explosion of inventions that changed the face of the world forever. Today, change is occurring at such a rapid rate that it is quite reasonable to assume that something that was brand-new only a few years ago is now completely obsolete. No doubt, the computer on which I wrote this book is by now considered a dinosaur.

Think of all of the things that not that long ago were familiar household items but that today are completely foreign to many young people. For example, do you know what the following image is?

Those of us born before the 1970s should recognize this as the adapter used for 45 rpm records. If you were born after the 1970s, you probably don't even know what a 45 rpm record is! The point is, in just a matter of years, things can change so much that we can lose any knowledge or understanding of how things used to work.

Now, think of the Bible. We're no longer talking about a few short years or decades or even a few centuries. Much of the Bible was written more than two thousand years ago. If you think things have changed a great deal over the past few years, imagine how much has changed over the last two or three thousand years. Not to mention the fact that the Bible comes to us from a land several thousand miles away from where most of us live and was written in a language quite different from the one spoken in your home or around the water coolers in your office. It is no wonder that some of the following things found in the Bible are as strange to us as an 8-track tape or a mimeograph machine might seem to today's generation:

> A catechist was teaching Bible stories to her students, describing how Lot's wife looked back and turned into a pillar of salt. Little Jason interrupted, "My mommy looked back once while she was driving," he announced triumphantly, "and she turned into a telephone pole!"

ephah	myrrh	dromedary
cubit	lyre	scroll
manna	diadem	mammon
shekel	drachma	sackcloth

Those are just things. What about formerly well-known people and places?

Sadducees	Meribah	Lake of Gennesaret
Ephesus	Pharisees	Boaz
Esau	Zealots	Nicodemus
Capernaum	Jairus	Sanhedrin

It's no wonder that we sometimes get a little frustrated when we read the Bible and come across some of these words that may mean absolutely *nothing* to us. It is as though we are looking through someone else's photo album without them nearby to explain what and who we are looking at. Without some assistance, we will find ourselves scratching our heads and perhaps giving up. Fortunately, help is right at our fingertips. The Bible may seem to us like a time capsule that is difficult to understand in our contemporary times, but the secrets of the past can be revealed to us in a variety of ways. Prepare to enter the world of footnotes, cross-references, concordances, and commentaries.

Try testing your biblical knowledge of some of the items mentioned in the previous lists.

Quiz

Test your knowledge of these biblical people, places, and things. The answers can be found at the bottom of the quiz.

1. An *ephah* is
- **a)** a type of rough adobe house lived in by Ephesians
- **b)** a unit of measure equal to one yard
- **c)** a dry measure equal to slightly more than a bushel
- **d)** the headscarf worn by unmarried Jewish women

2. *Manna* is
- **a)** the Hebrew word for "man"
- **b)** the substance the Israelites ate in the desert
- **c)** the town where Zacchaeus lived
- **d)** money or material things

3. A *drachma* is
- **a)** another name for a camel
- **b)** an ancient Greek silver coin
- **c)** one of the main items of property a bride brings to a marriage
- **d)** a turbanlike crown

4. A *lyre* is
- **a)** a stringed instrument similar to a harp
- **b)** a wineskin made from the stomach of a goat
- **c)** a form of Roman currency
- **d)** a wind instrument similar to a flute

5. A *scroll* is
- **a)** the name given to a Jewish priest
- **b)** Greek for "synagogue"
- **c)** a unit of measure equal to a foot
- **d)** a roll of papyrus, parchment, or leather used for writing

6. *Esau* refers to
  a) the village where Jesus raised Lazarus from the dead
  b) the name of a temple official
  c) the name of Jacob's brother
  d) the name of one of the twelve apostles

7. *Jairus* was the name of
  a) the man whose daughter Jesus raised from the dead
  b) the tax collector Jesus called down from the tree
  c) the town toward which the two disciples walked when Jesus appeared to them
  d) Moses's father-in-law

8. The *Sadducees* were
  a) a fourth-century BC Egyptian dynasty
  b) people who were very sad, you see?
  c) a separatist sect living in the desert
  d) a priestly aristocracy from which came the high priest

9. *Nicodemus* was
  a) a member of the Sanhedrin who came to Jesus at night
  b) one of the criminals crucified next to Jesus
  c) the high priest who sent Jesus to Pilate
  d) the name of the first Gentile converted by Paul

10. *Ephesus* was the name of
  a) the town whose walls fell down at the trumpet's blast
  b) one of the twelve apostles, "Peter," in Greek
  c) the city to which Paul addressed his letter to the Ephesians
  d) one of the twelve tribes of Israel

Quiz Answers

1. c; **2.** b; **3.** b; **4.** a; **5.** d; **6.** c; **7.** a; **8.** d; **9.** a; **10.** c.

Footnotes, Cross-References, Concordances, and Commentaries to the Rescue

Here's a Bible passage from the book of Deuteronomy concerning a law of marriage, which at first glance may seem difficult to understand. Read it over and see how much of it makes sense to you.

> 5 When brothers live together and one of them dies without a son, the widow of the deceased shall not marry anyone outside the family; but her husband's brother shall go to her and perform the duty of a brother-in-law by marrying her. 6 The first-born son she bears shall continue the line of the deceased brother, that his name may not be blotted out from Israel. 7 If, however, a man does not care to marry his brother's wife, she shall go up to the elders at the gate and declare, "My brother-in-law does not intend to perform his duty toward me and refuses to perpetuate his brother's name in Israel." 8 Thereupon the elders of his city shall summon him and admonish him. If he persists in saying , "I am not willing to marry her," 9* his sister-in-law, in the presence of the elders, shall go up to him and strip his sandal from his foot and spit in his face, saying publicly, "This is how one should be treated who will not build up his brother's family!" 10 And his lineage shall be spoken of in Israel as "the family of the man stripped of his sandal." (Dt 25:5–10, NAB)

What's going on here? How do we understand this passage? What does it mean to us today? Where do we go for help?

The idea of spitting in someone's face is easily understood and even today would be seen as a humiliating gesture. But, what's all this about stripping a man of his sandal? It seems far worse to have someone spit in your face than to take away a shoe. Yet, this passage tells us that the people of Israel will remember the ne'er-do-well brother-in-law, *not* as the one who had his face spat upon, but as the "man *stripped of his sandal.*" What's going on here? How do we understand this passage? What does it mean to us today? Where do we go for help?

The answer may lie in your Bible at the bottom of the page on which this passage is located (depending on which version of the Bible you're using). You'll notice that in this translation, verse 9 has an asterisk next to the verse number. This symbol indicates that there is additional information about this verse in a footnote. (Be aware that while different Bibles use different symbols to indicate a footnote, the most common symbols are an asterisk or consecutive letters of the alphabet.) So what's with the sandal? Here's the footnote for verse 9 in the New American Bible.

> 25:9 The penalty decreed for a man who refuses to comply with this law of family loyalty is public disgrace (the widow is to *spit in his face* [emphasis added]) and the curse of poverty; sandals were proverbially a man's cheapest possession (cf., Am 2:6; 8:6), and therefore "a man without sandals" was the poorest of the poor. (NAB)

Aha. Now, we are getting somewhere. Here's an example of a phrase that meant one thing to certain people a few thousand years ago but holds little meaning for us today. Yet, when we read the footnote provided for this passage, we see clearly how this act of removing a man's sandal was understood as a symbol of disgrace and a curse. Further, this footnote gives a cross-reference to the book of Amos. The abbreviation *cf.* (Latin for "compare") in the footnote indicates another passage that we should look up. If we find Amos 2:6 we discover the following quote:

Copyright © Doug Hall, 1991. Used by Permission.

By the time he realized the danger, Carl had developed a compulsive chain-reference habit.

"Thus says the Lord: / For three crimes of Israel, and for four, / I will not revoke my word; / Because they sell the just man for silver, / and the poor man for a pair of sandals." Likewise, in Amos 8:6 we find this: "We will buy the lowly man for silver, / and the poor man for a pair of sandals (NAB)."

The footnote and the cross-references provide readers with a clearer understanding of why this action of stripping a man of his sandal would be seen as such a powerful gesture. With this knowledge, we can go back to the original passage and reread it with a fuller understanding of what it meant to the people of Israel and of the role that the Law had in their lives.

Reading footnotes and cross-references may seem like a lot of work, but it is well worth it if we remember that we are reading the story of *our* salvation history. There are other payoffs as well. Once you look up a footnote or a cross-reference, you come away with an understanding that deepens your overall comprehension of the Bible because chances are, if you bump into a confusing word or phrase in one passage, it will come up in another. For example, take a look at the following passage that you've probably read numerous times: "As the people were filled with expectation, and all were questioning in their hearts concerning John, whether he might be the Messiah, John answered all of them by saying, 'I baptize you with water; but one who is more powerful than I is coming; I am not worthy to untie the thong of his sandals. He will baptize you with the Holy Spirit and fire'" (Lk 3:15–16). Now that our research has revealed that a man's sandal was his cheapest possession, we see how profound John the Baptist's statement is: he declares himself unworthy to touch Jesus' cheapest possession, namely, his sandal. By the way, we've also discovered a response to the age-old complaint of many Christians who feel that reading the Old Testament is a waste of time, thinking that it has nothing to teach us about Jesus. Think again. The Old Testament understanding of a man's sandal as his cheapest possession sheds light on this New Testament passage concerning John the Baptist's perspective on Jesus.

Footnotes provide us with many different types of information. Here are some examples:

- the meaning(s) of a word or phrase
- the historical setting of a story
- geographical locations

> "Most people are bothered by those passages of Scripture they do not understand, but the passages that bother me are those I do understand."
> —MARK TWAIN

- important dates
- how certain stories and people are related
- references to other languages and an explanation of nuances in the original language that may be lost in the translation to English
- theological insight
- patterns to watch for
- customs and traditions of biblical peoples
- cross-references to similar occurrences of the same word, phrase, person, or situation

Footnotes provide a tool for scraping away centuries of "dirt and mud" to discover the true meaning of the Word of God. By using footnotes, you will be able to see many passages in the Bible in a whole new light. Footnotes didn't just appear in the Bible. We can thank Scripture scholars and archeologists who have literally dug and scraped until they painstakingly uncovered insights into the past that allow us to bring the Word of God to the present and carry it into the future. (For that reason, it's important to have a Bible that incorporates the best of Catholic Scripture scholarship. But we'll talk more about selecting a Bible later.)

Now, let's practice looking up some footnotes.

Read the following Scripture stories along with any footnotes that are provided with the text. Make a brief list of any new information you learn.

- Noah's ark (Gn 6:5–22)
- the Covenant with Abram (Gn 15)
- the call of Moses (Ex 3:4–22)
- Psalm 22
- the genealogy of Jesus and the birth of Jesus (Mt 1)
- the vocation of Saul (Acts 9:1–30)
- the woman and the dragon (Rv 12)

Learning to Cross-Reference

Footnotes may seem confusing at first glance until we learn how to find the information tied to these little symbols. In the same way, cross-references may look extremely off-putting. We may find a section of text near the bottom of our Bible page that contains an extensive list of numbers or letters and Bible passages. Here's an example of what it may look like in your Bible.

---

a Prv 8:14f. *b* Prv 1:6; Sir 39:1ff; 42:19f; Dn 2:21. *c* 1Kgs 3:28; Jb 29:8ff, 20f. *d* Sir 15:6; 41:12f; Is 56:5.

What's all this, then? Once again, you need to figure out which symbols your Bible is using. In the New American Bible (NAB), lowercase, italicized letters found in the text indicate a cross-reference, or where you can find another passage dealing with the same or related topic, story, character, etc. For example, if you were to read in the NAB version of the Gospel of John about Jesus' arrest, you will find at the end of Jn 18:1, a lowercase, italicized *n* indicating a cross-reference. In the list of cross-references, you will find that something related to this passage may be found in the following places:

> 2 Sm 15:23
> Mt 26:30-36
> Mk 14:26-32
> Lk 22:39

By looking up the cross-references, you can compare how different books of the Bible tell the same story or echo a similar event. For example, in the following passage in Luke, chapter 4, describing Jesus' appearance in the synagogue at Nazareth, notice the indication of a cross-reference in the text that Jesus reads from the scroll of Isaiah:

18 The spirit of the Lord is upon me,
  because he has anointed me
    to bring glad tidings to the poor. *z*
He has sent me to proclaim liberty to captives
  and recovery of sight to the blind,
    to let the oppressed go free,
19 and to proclaim a year acceptable to the Lord. (NAB)

A Footnote About Footnotes

Recall our earlier discussion about how different Bibles abbreviate books differently. The same caution needs to be made here about cross-references and footnotes. Different translations or editions of the Bible may have a different approach to cross-references. Some editions will list cross-references in the column directly next to the text. Others will simply list cross-references at the bottom of the page without using any symbols. Still others may not even use cross-references at all. By the same token, different Bibles approach footnotes in a variety of ways. Some Bibles footnote extensively, others very little. Some use symbols while others use letters. The important thing is to read the introductory pages of your Bible to identify how that Bible uses cross-references and footnotes.

If you are a curious reader, you may ask yourself, "Where in Isaiah can I find that passage?" Behold cross-reference z. In the cross-reference section, look for the letter z. You'll find this cross-reference: Is 61:1–2; 58:6.

Because you know how to read Scripture citations properly and can use your abbreviation list in the table of contents, you know that you are looking for Isaiah, chapter 61, verses 1 and 2. Likewise, if you happen to be reading Is 61:1–2 and think to yourself, "This sounds familiar. Didn't Jesus say these words?" the cross-reference on Is 61:1 will direct you to look at Lk 4:18. Isn't *that* convenient?

Cross-references will send you traveling all over the Bible, enabling you to make more connections than the electrical wiring in your house. Much like footnotes, by using cross-references, you will be able to unleash the full power of God's Word by opening doors from one passage to another and from one insight to another.

But what happens when our footnotes and cross-references aren't enough?

To practice, look up the cross-references given in your Bible for the following Gospel stories from Matthew:

- the birth of Jesus (Mt 1:20)
- the baptism of Jesus (Mt 3:13)
- the temptation of Jesus (Mt 4:1)
- the Golden Rule (Mt 7:12)
- Jesus feeds five thousand (Mt 14:13)
- the entry into Jerusalem (Mt 21:1)
- the Holy Eucharist (Mt 26:26)
- the Agony in the Garden (Mt 26:36)
- the women at the tomb (Mt 28:1)

Biblical Concordances and Dictionaries

Recall our earlier discussion of bibliaphobia. We addressed the idea that one of the reasons many of us are afraid of the Bible is its length. Most Bibles are between one and two thousand pages in length with miniscule print. Add to that the dizzying number of footnotes and cross-references, and each page can become quite involved. What's truly amazing is that despite all of the information given in the footnotes and cross-references, they only scratch the surface of the background information that could be given for each Scripture passage. If some kind of footnote or cross-reference were included for every name, date, and location in the Bible, it would increase the length of our Bibles from one or two thousand pages to ten or twenty thousand pages. For that reason, only the most essential information is given to us right in our Bibles. Additional information is available in what we call a biblical concordance (sometimes referred to as a dictionary concordance). Today, a wide variety of biblical concordances are available not only in book form but also on CD and online. The following list is an example of the kinds of information you're likely to find in a concordance:

- literally tens of thousands of subject entries

- nearly a million words that occur in the Bible

- every name in the Bible

- descriptions of biblical places and of the daily life of the Hebrew people

- summaries of each book of the Bible

- historical background

At one time, biblical concordances were primarily a tool for Scripture scholars and theology majors. Today, it is not necessary for the average Catholic to enroll in university theology classes to gain access to biblical information. Scholars have already done that work for us and have placed the fruits of their labor at our fingertips in these very valuable volumes, which are available at most bookstores and online. See the annotated bibliography for Catholic Scripture study on page 114 for suggested titles. With a concordance at our side, each time we read the Bible it is as though we have a Scripture scholar sitting beside us to answer our every question.

Biblical Commentaries

Finally, even with footnotes, cross-references, and concordance information, sometimes we still need assistance in understanding the meaning and significance of specific passages within the context of the whole chapter, book, testament, or Bible. At times like this, we need the assistance of biblical commentaries. Commentaries are essays that lead us chapter by chapter and verse by verse through each book of the Bible, providing us with a more detailed and holistic explanation of the Scripture passages we are reading. Commentaries are very helpful for those involved in Scripture study, preaching, pastoral ministry,

"I've dated guys who carried Bibles, but never anyone who carried a twelve volume commentary."

Copyright © Doug Hall, 1991. Used by Permission.

or catechesis. However, personal prayer can be greatly enhanced as well by reading biblical commentaries. After reading a Scripture passage, it is often helpful to browse through a commentary before returning to the passage and prayerfully rereading it (more on how to prayerfully read the Bible in chapter 9). With the depth and background provided by the commentary, the Word of God comes to life for us in a way that was not previously possible. Using a commentary to enhance our personal Scripture study and prayer is like plugging in an electrical device that previously did not work—the potential was there all along but the connection needed to be made! (See the annotated bibliography for Catholic Scripture study on page 114 for suggested titles.)

Using Your "Archeological" Tools

If we think of the Bible as a time capsule that contains valuable and meaningful treasures buried under centuries of dirt and mud, then we should think of footnotes, cross-references, concordances, and commentaries as the archeological tools we need to scrape away that which prevents us from encountering the full power of God's Word. With these tools at our fingertips, we are now ready to forge ahead and make some startling discoveries about the Bible and how it can make a profound impact on our daily living.

Questions for Reflection and Discussion

- If you were to assemble a time capsule that captured the most significant and essential events, people, fads, news stories, and so on of the past year, what would you include?

- If you assembled such a time capsule, what might people one hundred years from now have difficulty recognizing or understanding?

- Name something you have that is now obsolete but was considered "state of the art" only a short time ago.

- What part of the Bible have you had the most difficulty understanding?

- Browse through the Bible and search out a few footnotes. What is something you learned from reading a footnote that you did not know before?

- Do the same with a few cross-references. What is something you learned about a passage by comparing its cross-references?

- In what ways can a biblical concordance enhance your personal study of the Bible?

- How can biblical commentaries be of assistance to you in your understanding of the Bible?

Chapter Six

Recognizing Symbolic Language in the Bible

Do you know what the following symbols represent?

A.   **B.**  **C.**

If you knew the language of blueprints, you would know that **A** represents a pair of windows, **B** represents bi-fold doors, and **C** represents finished wood. A little training in how to read blueprints and it's as if you can read and speak another language. When it comes to reading and understanding the Bible, we need to be able to decipher some of the symbolic language that it contains.

So, then, is it true that

- God created the world in seven days?
- Adam lived to be 930 years old?
- Noah built an ark and got two of *every* animal to board it?
- Jonah was swallowed by a large fish?
- the walls of Jericho fell at the blast of a trumpet?
- Samson lost all of his physical strength when he got his hair cut?
- David slew a giant named Goliath with a slingshot?
- Jesus survived forty days and forty nights in the desert without food?
- tongues of fire appeared over the apostles at the feast of Pentecost?
- Only 144,000 will be saved at the end of the world?

However, since God speaks in Sacred Scripture through men in human fashion, the interpreter of Sacred Scripture, in order to see clearly what God wanted to communicate to us, should carefully investigate what meaning the sacred writers really intended, and what God wanted to manifest by means of their words. (*Dei Verbum*, 12)

Facts in the Bible

Although biblical authors were not primarily concerned with fact telling, the fact is, the Bible is a rich resource of historical data. In many cases, archeology has verified the existence of people, places, and events mentioned in the Bible. One of the first "finds" took place in 1843 when Paul-Émile Botta uncovered some tablets in Iraq on which the name Sar-gin was inscribed. This inscription was a reference to Sargon, the King of Assyria, who is mentioned in Isaiah 20:1. Since then, archeology has confirmed the existence of a number of biblical references including the cities of Ur, Nineveh, and Jericho, as well as the existence of the Hittites, the fall of the northern kingdom of Israel, and much more. While it is true that there are many historical discrepancies when it comes to biblical facts, the Bible remains a treasury of historical information.

How are we to understand some of these passages in the Bible? We may believe that the events listed above happened (or will happen) precisely the way the Bible describes them. Such an approach affirms the awesome and almighty power of God, who can accomplish anything God wants. It may also lead us to wonder why such extraordinary events no longer seem to occur today in the same manner. Did God interact differently with the world in biblical times? On the other hand, we may conclude that these events did not occur exactly the way the Bible describes them and are just *stories*. This conclusion explains why God seemed a little more "hands on" back then. Unfortunately, this approach may also lead us to conclude that the Bible is simply a collection of fables and fairy tales, to be lumped together with those of Aesop and the Brothers Grimm.

How we answer this question of "truth" is at the very core of our faith and our understanding of how God communicates with us in life as well as through Sacred Scripture. Without further ado, allow me to propose an answer that captures the essence of the Catholic approach to understanding the Bible: everything in the Bible is *true*—but not necessarily *fact*.

The way this answer is phrased is critical. Let there be no doubt that the Bible communicates the absolute truth of God. At the same time, understand that truth and fact are not the same thing! This answer is not meant to be tricky or gimmicky. It is intended to be a profound statement to all those who question whether or not the Bible is God's Word or just a collection of stories. Make no mistake about it, the Bible is the Word of God and everything in it conveys truth. Equally as important, this answer is offered as a more authentic, orthodox, and effective reply than the unfortunate and damaging "No, these things didn't really happen. They're just stories." Too many well-intentioned pastors, teachers, catechists, and pastoral ministers have used this reckless reply in their attempts to provide their students and parishioners with a

Everything in the Bible is *true*—but not necessarily *fact*.

more mature and contemporary approach to the Bible. Instead of leading people to a deeper understanding of the Bible, the "they're just stories" approach minimizes the power of God's Word, often leading people to abandon the Bible.

Finally, the caveat included in the statement above (but not necessarily *fact*) accomplishes two things. First, it reminds us that we can depend on the historicity of much of the Bible. With the help of Scripture scholars and the guidance of the Church, we are able to identify those occasional passages that, while conveying truth, may not be relating facts. Second, it speaks to those who might espouse a fundamentalist (literal) approach to the Bible that would lead people to a narrow-minded approach to God's Word. While a literal approach to the Bible emphasizes the power of God in biblical stories, it creates a chasm between those stories and our own contemporary personal experience (e.g., God used to do things like part the waters of the Red Sea, but he doesn't seem to do things like that anymore), thus calling into question the power of God in our everyday life. When we say that everything in the Bible is true, but not necessarily fact, we do not diminish the power of God in either the Bible or our experience. Likewise, we do not diminish the importance of the Bible but instead raise it up to a new height of importance, challenging readers and believers to approach it in a manner in which no other literature is approached. God's Library is no ordinary library, and its contents cannot be understood in the same way that other books are understood.

Understanding Myth in a Literal Society

In order to truly understand the Bible, we need to go back and understand the culture in which it was written—a culture that understood stories and the concept of myth in a much different way than we tend to understand them today. We live in a very literal culture. Through science, we have the power to prove almost anything. If something cannot be proven, it is considered false. Today, when we refer to something

Copyright © Doug Hall, 1991. Used by Permission.

"Sometimes Greg encounters more truth than he can handle."

as a story, we are suggesting that what is being communicated is not true. Likewise, our use of the word *myth* carries very negative connotations. When someone concocts a tall tale, we call it a myth. As a result, the word *myth* is almost synonymous with the words *lie* and *falsehood*.

Not so in biblical culture.

The difference between contemporary cultures and cultures of biblical times can be traced to an understanding of the differences between truth and fact. In the cultures of biblical times, stories and myth were seen as the vehicles by which the most essential and sacred truths of a people were communicated and passed on. Scientific proof was not available, nor was it needed in order to pass on what the heart held as absolute and essential. Today, unless something is substantiated by facts, we consider it false. In biblical times, truth could be conveyed whether or not the facts were all straight. For this reason, it is critical for Bible readers to rely on the insights of Scripture scholars who can shed light on the original author's intent and help us sort out what was intended to be presented as fact and what wasn't. We'll talk more about this in the next chapter.

Since society in biblical times did not base its sense of truth on literal interpretation, facts were often of secondary importance. In other words, biblical cultures understood that something can be true but need not be a fact! At first, this may sound outrageous, but a closer look at our own culture and use of language reveals that we know exactly how to find truth in something that isn't factual. Read the following paragraph and pay attention to the phrases in italics.

> My kids are *driving me up the wall*. There I was, trying to get to church on time, and these little *rugrats* were *tearing up the place*. I was *pulling my hair out* to keep some kind of order in the house and they didn't *give a hoot*. To *top it all off*, when we left the house, it was *raining cats and dogs*. Since I left my umbrella at work, *I was up the creek without a paddle*. So I had to *hotfoot* it to the car while *juggling* these two kids. Naturally, we *drowned*. Then, when we got to within a block of church, this train with a *billion* cars *crawled* across the street at about *two feet an hour*. I *blew my top*. After waiting there about *three days*, we finally got to church and sat down just as Father was giving a talk about getting to church on time. *I just about died!*

What you've just read is a true story, in that the events described truly occurred. However, many of the phrases used to describe these events are not at all factual. As long as you understand the use of figurative language, you have no problem accepting the story as true. You would never pause to ask, "Is it true that cats and dogs were falling from the sky?" The use of the phrase *cats and dogs* conveys truth without using fact. As long as you

> **It is critical for Bible readers to rely on the insights of Scripture scholars who can shed light on the original author's intent and help us sort out what was intended to be presented as fact and what wasn't.**

understand figurative language, the hyperbole of the language doesn't faze you. It is this understanding of figurative language that allows us to conclude that everything in the Bible is true, but not everything in the Bible is a fact. With this in mind, let's take a closer look at some examples from Scripture.

Is it true that Adam lived to be 930 years old? If you understand that the biblical authors use age in the Old Testament to make a point, you'll get it. In Jewish culture (as in many others), to live a long life is considered to be a blessing from God. Adam, who was the father of all, was truly blessed and his age represents that. As the stories in Genesis continue on, the ages decrease as the sinfulness of humankind escalates. The use of age here is not intended to represent fact but to convey truth: God's blessing is gradually being rejected by men and women who are in need of salvation.

How Can We Tell When Figurative Language Is Being Used?

Knowing that the Bible occasionally uses figurative language is one thing. Knowing *when* the Bible is using figurative language is another. How can the average lay Bible reader know? We are not free to apply whatever meaning we choose to any Scripture passage. When you encounter a Bible passage that you think may be using figurative language, consider the following:

- look at the context of the passage
- use your own common sense and personal experience (is it suggesting what seems to be an impossibility, such as Adam living to be 930 years old?)
- consider your own knowledge of language and grammar (simile, metaphor, allegory, hyperbole, and so on)
- look for footnotes about the passage
- focus on the author's overall intent
- read a commentary about the passage

In general, approach the words of the Bible in their literal sense unless there is some convincing reason to consider it otherwise. And remember, behind every figure of speech, you will find a literal meaning. Even though facts may not be present in a given Scripture passage, you are encountering God's truth!

Is it true that Noah built an ark and got two of every species of animal on board to survive a flood that washed out all of humankind? There most likely was a devastating flood that wiped out vast areas of the earth in Old Testament times. Archeological data and the existence of similar catastrophic flood stories in various cultures and religious traditions seem to support this. Consider this: because of mass communication and technology, our world has been transformed into a global village. When something happens on one side of the world, the rest of the world can watch it on the news.

In primitive cultures, this was not true. What people perceived as the "world" was restricted by a limited knowledge of geography. A devastating flood could easily have wiped out the "world" as it was known at the time by a particular culture. Such tragedies were often seen as punishment from God. Perhaps a just man named Noah did survive such a flood by sheltering his family and his farm animals on a large boat. We don't know the facts. However, we do know that this is a true story. The story teaches us the sacred and essential truth that humankind will drown in sinfulness. The only thing that will keep one afloat is to live an upright life. Sinfulness is punished and goodness is saved. God replenishes that which God has created. Perhaps someday, someone will find Noah's ark and prove that the story is indeed factual. In the meantime, we already know that it's true.

> **"The Bible shows the way to go to heaven, not the way the heavens go."**
> —GALILEO GALILEI

Is it true that the Garden of Eden exists? In the book of Genesis, we are told that the Garden of Eden exists where four rivers meet: the Pishon, the Gihon, the Tigris, and the Euphrates. All you need to do is discover where these four rivers meet and you will have discovered the Garden of Eden. The only problem is that these four rivers do not meet. Is the Bible lying to us? Is the Bible false? No. These four rivers *do* meet—in the world of myth. The biblical author is alerting us to the fact that this story is *sacred*. The reader is being forewarned: prepare to enter into sacred space and confront an essential truth of life.

Is it true that God created the world in seven days? If we believe the creation story literally, what do we do about the big bang and evolution? If we believe the big bang theory and the theory of evolution, does that make the Bible's version false? No. We don't have to take sides. The Bible story of creation in seven days is a true story. Likewise, the second story of creation found in Genesis, chapter 2, is *also* true. The Bible itself gives us two stories—which is true? They both are. Even though the *facts* of the two stories conflict, they both teach us sacred and essential truths: creation comes from God; all of creation is good and blessed; man and woman are made in the image of God; humankind is responsible for caring for creation; and the idea of resting once per week is divine. As for the facts concerning the actual process of creation—we don't know. We weren't there when it happened. However, the biblical stories of creation and the scientific theories of the big bang and evolution are not mutually exclusive. As one bumper sticker puts it: "The Big Bang Theory: God said BANG! and it happened!"

"I've Been in the Belly of the Whale!"

Once, after I explained to a group of adults how the Jonah story is true though not necessarily fact, a woman came up to me with tears in her eyes. She said that she understood what the story was teaching because she had "been in the belly of the whale." She explained that she was in a 12-step program recovering from an addiction and said that hitting rock bottom and being in complete darkness was like being in the belly of the whale. Now, she realized that if she followed God's will instead of trying to run and hide from it, conversion would be possible. She knew without a doubt that the Jonah story is true. She recognized that the miracle in the story is not that God once provided a huge fish to swallow Jonah, but that God can change your heart, if you stop running.

Is it true that Jonah was swallowed by a large fish? Like every story in the Bible, we need to remind ourselves that the story of Jonah is not just about a character that lived long ago and far away, it is our story. Every Bible story is somehow the story of your life and my life. The story of Jonah is not a story about whether a man can factually survive in the belly of a large fish for three days, but a story about what happens when you and I try to run away from God's call and God's will. Jonah was called by God to preach to the people of Nineveh and call them to repentance. He didn't want to do that. So, in the great tradition

"Maybe you should have accepted that call to Schenectady."

of Adam and Eve, he tried to run and hide, eventually finding himself in the belly of a large fish for three days before coming to his senses. This true story teaches us that when we run from God, we encounter storms, darkness, and isolation, and that in our isolation, God can and will find us. God does not give up easily.

Is it true that Jesus went forty days and forty nights in the desert without eating any food? Jesus is the Son of God and can perform miracles beyond explanation. At the same time, he is fully human. No human can survive a month and ten days in the desert without some kind of food. Yet, this is a true story. We mentioned a few moments ago that it's important to pay attention to the use of numbers in the Bible. Here we have forty days and forty nights. (Where have you seen this number used before?) The number forty is highly symbolic. It communicates the idea of a significant period of time. Recall that the people of Israel passed through the waters of the Red Sea and spent forty years wandering through the desert, often tempted because of lack of food. Jesus now has passed through the waters of his baptism and is led into the desert where he, too, is tempted. Israel failed their test. Jesus is triumphant. The truth of this story is that for a significant period of time, reminiscent of the time that Israel spent in the desert, Jesus faced temptation regarding mankind's true source of nourishment and well-being. He resists temptation and places his trust in the Father who alone is the source of nourishment and well-being. We, too, have crossed through the waters of Baptism and endure significant periods of dryness during which we grapple with the question of our true source of nourishment and well-being. Jesus' experience provides us with the answer.

Flying made Judy very, very nervous, so she always took her Bible along with her to read, as it helped relax her. One time, the man she was sitting next to saw her pull out her Bible. He gave a little chuckle and smirk and asked, "You don't really believe all that stuff in there, do you?" Judy replied, "Of course I do. It is the Bible." He said, "Well, what about that guy that was swallowed by that whale?" Judy replied, "Oh, Jonah. Yes, I believe that, it is in the Bible." He asked, "Well, how do you suppose he survived all that time inside the whale?" Judy said, "Well, I don't really know. I guess when I get to Heaven, I will ask him." "What if he isn't in Heaven?" the man asked sarcastically. "Then you can ask him," replied Judy.

Was it light or was it dark? The Gospel of Mark tells us that the women came to the tomb on that first Easter morning "very early on the first day of the week, when the sun had risen" (Mk 16:2). The Gospel of John tells us that they came upon the tomb "while it was still dark" (Jn 20:1). This conflict may cause us trouble if we are looking for the literal time of the Resurrection. When did they come to the tomb? If the sun had risen, it would be bright and not still dark. Which story is true? They both are. The Gospel of John uses the images of light and dark throughout: "the light shines in the darkness" (1:5), "But those who do what is true come to the light" (3:21), "I am the light of the world" (9:5), "I have come as light into the world" (12:46). It makes sense to have the women arrive at the tomb "while it was still dark," to reinforce the image that the people who "walk in darkness" will soon see "a great light" (also reminiscent of Isaiah 9:1). The fact that these two stories describe the same event, yet use different "facts," reinforces the notion that the authors are not as concerned with literal facts as we are today but are instead concerned with communicating the truth—namely, that Jesus, the light of the world, is risen.

Was it on the mount or on the plain? We are all familiar with Jesus' famous discourse referred to as the Beatitudes (i.e., Blessed are the poor in spirit . . .). Interestingly enough, Matthew's Gospel tells us that Jesus delivered this sermon on "the mountain" (mount) while Luke's Gospel tells us that it was delivered on "level ground" (plain). Simply put, a mount is not a plain. Which story is true? Once again, both. The authors are not concerned with the fact of where Jesus stood but instead with the truth of his teaching. Matthew's Gospel is written for an audience that was primarily Jewish. A Jewish audience would need a great deal of convincing to believe that Jesus was a greater prophet than Moses. What better way to do this than to have Jesus deliver his new "commandments" from atop a mountain, just as Moses received the Ten Commandments on Mount Sinai? The facts of where Jesus actually stood are overpowered by the truth being communicated here: Jesus is a prophet far greater than even Moses.

But Wait, There's More!

We've just skimmed the surface of how we can recognize truth and fact in the Bible. We're going to see in the next chapter that the biblical authors often provide us with clues that they are dabbling in figurative language. Like the rumble strips on the side of the highway that alert us to pay closer attention to the road, these biblical clues let us know that we need to be alert to the deeper meaning of the upcoming passage.

Questions for Reflection and Discussion

- In your own words, describe the difference between truth and fact. What are some examples from everyday language?

- A clever Scripture professor once said, "Everything in the Bible is true . . . and some of them actually happened." What does this mean? How does it compare with the statement we've used? (Everything in the Bible is true, but not necessarily fact.)

- After reading this chapter, how would you respond to someone who asks you a question like: "Did Adam and Eve really exist?" or "Was there really a Noah's ark?"

- After reading this chapter, how would you respond to someone who accuses you of making the Bible sound like a fairy tale by all this talk about the difference between truth and fact?

- For a good laugh, rent the movie *Airplane* and make a list of all the figurative language that is portrayed literally. Use this as an exercise in illustrating how complex language can be. For children, locate a copy of *Amelia Bedelia*, which also illustrates how comical it can be to take something literally that is meant to be understood figuratively.

Chapter Seven

Do the Math—
Numbers in the Bible

A critical skill required in reading blueprints is a basic understanding of math functions. Numbers—dimensions and measurements—play a significant role in blueprints. Likewise, numbers (not the book of Numbers!) play a significant role in the Bible. Just as a craftsman needs to know what to do with numbers in a blueprint, we need to know what to make of the various usages of numbers that appear throughout the Bible.

As you read the Bible, pay close attention to the use of numbers and locations. References to numbers and locations are often a clue to some deeper symbolic meaning. While archeology has substantiated many historical, geographical, and numerical references in the Bible, quite often the authors were not as interested in the facts as we tend to be but were instead using numbers and locations as a tool for communicating something symbolic. Let's take a closer look at each of these.

What is the literal sense of a passage is not always as obvious in the speeches and writings of the ancient authors of the East, as it is in the works of our own time. For what they wished to express is not to be determined by the rules of grammar and philology alone, nor solely by the context; the interpreter must, as it were, go back wholly in spirit to those remote centuries of the East and with the aid of history, archaeology, ethnology, and other sciences, accurately determine what modes of writing, so to speak, the authors of that ancient period would be likely to use, and in fact did use. (*Divino Afflante Spiritu*, 35)

The Number Forty

Guess what the answer is to all of the following questions:

- How many days and nights did it rain for Noah?
- How many days did it take to embalm Jacob?
- How many years old were Jacob and Esau when they each got married?
- How many years did the Israelites wander through the desert?
- How many years did both David and Solomon rule as king?
- How many years old was Moses when he slew an Egyptian?
- How many years later did Moses encounter the burning bush?
- How many days was Moses on the mountaintop before he came down with the Commandments?
- How many days did it take Moses's scouts to reconnoiter the land of Canaan?
- How many days and nights did Goliath take his stand before meeting up with David?
- How many days and nights did Elijah walk, strengthened by the food and drink he received?
- How many days' warning did Jonah give the people of Nineveh?
- How many days and nights did Jesus spend in the desert without food?
- How many days did Jesus remain with his disciples after his Resurrection?

The answer to all of the above: forty!

Numbers

The biblical authors loved numbers. Some numbers are good. Some are bad. Some numbers are repeated so often that we can rightly become a bit suspicious. We've already talked a little about the number forty. You might be surprised to know that the number forty occurs nearly two hundred times in the Bible. This is a clue that it is being used as a symbol and not strictly to communicate fact. Deuteronomy 8:2 tells us about the significance of the number forty. "Remember the long way that the LORD your God has led you these forty years in the wilderness, in order to humble you, testing you to know what was in your heart, whether or not you would keep his commandments." In other words, the number forty represents a significant period of time during which a person's faithfulness is tested and can be judged or determined. Other numbers are used frequently in the Bible to convey symbolic meaning.

3 The number three appears hundreds of times in the Bible. In biblical tradition, it is always on the third day that God saves. The angel intervened to stop Abraham from sacrificing Isaac on the third day. After three days in the desert without water, God provided fresh water through Moses. The prophet Hosea says, "After two days he will revive us; / on the third day he will raise us up / to live in his presence" (6:2). Jonah emerged from the large fish on the third day. Paul regained his sight on the third day. Mary and Joseph found the twelve-year-old Jesus in the temple on the third day. Jesus fed four thousand people after they had been with him for three days with nothing to eat.

> **The bottom line to all this is that numbers are a clue to the reader: pay attention and look for the deeper meaning. Look for the truth being communicated.**

Jesus rose from the dead on the third day. The book of Exodus gives us a clue about the significance of the third day when it says, "Go to the people and consecrate them today and tomorrow. Have them wash their clothes and prepare for the third day, because on the third day the LORD will come down upon Mount Sinai in the sight of all the people. On the morning of the third day there was thunder and lightning, as well as a thick cloud on the mountain, and a blast of a trumpet so loud that all the people who were in the camp trembled. Now Mount Sinai was wrapped in smoke, because the LORD had descended upon it in fire . . ." (19:10–11, 16, 18). Needless to say, the number three is one of those good numbers in the Bible because God always comes through on the third day.

6 The number six, on the other hand, is not such a good number. Not that it's bad, but it tends to represent incompleteness. Noah was six hundred years old when the flood came. Pharaoh sent six hundred first-class chariots to chase after the Israelites. God worked for six days to create the heavens and the earth but blessed and made holy the seventh day for rest. Of course, in the book of Revelation, the "beast" is represented by the number 666. Think about that: three is a good number, representing completeness. Six represents incompleteness. Three sixes, or 666, represents complete incompleteness! In other words, the use of 666 in the book of Revelation is not some secret code to tell us who the Antichrist will be. It is simply a symbolic way of representing evil in whatever form it may take in any age.

7 The number seven—ah, back to the good numbers—tends to represent fullness or perfection. God rested on the seventh day. Noah took seven pairs of all clean animals aboard the ark. The walls of Jericho came tumbling down after seven days of trumpet playing. Jesus tells Peter to forgive his brother seventy times seven times. The book of Revelation speaks to the seven churches. The same book also tells us that the seventh trumpet will signal the end of the world. Whenever we encounter the number seven, it tends to be satisfying.

12 Last but not least is the number twelve. Twelve, of course, symbolizes first and foremost the fullness of the people of Israel, with its twelve tribes. The people of Israel discovered an oasis called Elim with twelve streams of water. Jesus, of course, had twelve apostles. And, once again, the book of Revelation tops it all off by telling us that one hundred forty-four thousand people will be saved at the end of the world. This number is divisible by twelve, representing twelve thousand from each of the twelve tribes of Israel—not a restrictive or exclusive number of people but an expansive and inclusive number. In other words, God wants all people to be saved. With this much use of the number twelve, we can be sure that we are dealing with metaphorical language and not facts. In other words, we don't know how many people will be saved at the end of the world, but the truth is that God's work will have reached its completion.

The bottom line to all this is that numbers are a clue to the reader: pay attention and look for the deeper meaning. Look for the truth being communicated.

Back to the Number Forty

Is it any coincidence that human pregnancy, on the average, lasts forty weeks? Could it be that this may be the reason for the significance of the number forty in the Bible? Pregnancy involves pain and growth that leads to the birth of new life. Many of the occurrences of the number forty in the Bible—Noah's ark, the wandering in the desert, Jesus' temptation in the desert—are stories of profound growth accompanied by pain, resulting in new life and a new beginning.

Locations

Many biblical references to locations have proven to be historically accurate. Archeologists have unearthed cities referred to in the Old Testament that were thought to be fictional or at least long gone. Many locations referred to still exist, some in a relatively unchanged state. On the other hand, we encounter many other references to locations that prove troublesome. We've already discussed the problem of the location of the Garden of Eden and the question of whether Jesus delivered the Beatitudes on a mount or on a plain. More questions may arise as we read. Was Jesus really born in Bethlehem? Did the Holy Family really hide in Egypt? Did Jesus travel to Jerusalem once as Matthew, Mark, and Luke tell us or three times as John indicates? (Notice the use of the number three here?) Why were the two disciples on the road to a place called Emmaus after Jesus' death?

The key here is to recall our discussion of the difference between truth and fact. The biblical authors were concerned with teaching truth. They were not historians or geographers and their use of locations is often as symbolic as their use of numbers. Locations conjure up images. Even today when someone names a location, people have a reaction, either positive or negative depending on what that location suggests. How are we to know how people in biblical times reacted to certain locations? Often, footnotes and commentaries will contain useful information. For now, here are a few clues about some places that we just mentioned.

Bethlehem The prophet Micah refers to Bethlehem saying, "But you, O Bethlehem of Ephrathah, / who are one of the little clans of Judah, / from you shall come forth for me / one who is to rule in Israel" (5:2). When the Gospels of Matthew and Luke tell us that Jesus was born in Bethlehem, they are teaching us the truth that Jesus is the ruler who has come from humble beginnings to become the shepherd of all Israel, thus fulfilling the hopes and expectations of God's people.

Egypt The Gospel of Matthew is the only Gospel that recounts the flight into Egypt. Recall that Matthew was writing for a predominantly Jewish audience familiar with the story of the Exodus. To such an audience, this reference would immediately summon images of the time that God called forth his people out of the land of Egypt. In the same way,

Jesus would now be seen as called by God out of the land of Egypt to form a new people. While there is much we don't know about Jesus' early life, we do know this: Jesus is he who is called to emancipate the new Israel (that means you and me) from the sin that enslaves us and lead us to the promised land of our salvation.

Jesus' Travels to Jerusalem Matthew, Mark, and Luke tell us that Jesus "cleansed" the Temple during his last days as part of his only journey to Jerusalem. John places this event near the beginning of his ministry and has Jesus traveling to Jerusalem a total of three times. These facts seem to conflict. The truth is, however, that Jerusalem and the Temple were seen as the center of Jewish life. John's Gospel was written at a time when Jewish Christians were experiencing the turmoil of being "thrown out" of their synagogues as the split between Jews and Jewish Christians deepened and grew acrimonious. John's chronology of Jesus' three visits to Jerusalem and his references to the cleansing of the Temple at the beginning of Jesus' ministry emphasize the truth that Jesus is the new center of God's presence in the world, replacing the Temple in Jerusalem that the Christians of John's time no longer had access to. And, since God saves on the third day, it makes sense that Jesus' saving action—his death and Resurrection—would occur on his third visit to Jerusalem.

Emmaus Where the heck is Emmaus and why are two disciples headed there after Jesus' tragic death? The fact is, very little is known about Emmaus. It seems to have absolutely no significance, and that's the point. After Jesus' death, the disciples were lost and directionless. The only important thing about the location of Emmaus is that the two disciples are headed *away* from Jerusalem. The disciples are attempting to leave behind the experience of Jesus' death. They don't know where they are headed as long as it is away from the past. After their encounter with the risen Jesus on the road to Emmaus, their destination changes: they make a 180-degree turn and head back to Jerusalem, back to where Jesus' death occurred. While we know little about a place called Emmaus, we do know the truth: when we are lost and without direction, we do not recognize the presence of the risen Lord in our midst. When we do encounter him in the sharing of God's Word and the breaking of the bread, our eyes are opened, and we can revisit the place of our pain with a new faith.

Personally, my favorite location reference is a little-known one found in the sixth chapter of Mark's Gospel. The chapter begins with Jesus and his disciples in Nazareth. Jesus encounters some difficulty in his own town. He proceeds to send out the twelve. After they come back reporting their success, Jesus invites them to an out-of-the-way place, a deserted region not far from the shore of the Sea of Galilee. In this deserted place, Jesus feeds five thousand people despite the apostles' reluctance. All of this is taking place on the western shore of the Sea of Galilee—Jewish territory. After this incident, Jesus tells the apostles to get in the boat and precede him to the other side of the lake toward Bethsaida—Gentile territory. That evening, the apostles do so, but encounter their own turbulence as they try to row with the wind against them. Between three and six in the morning (note: they've been rowing since evening—a total of between nine and twelve hours), Jesus comes walking on the water toward them. After he gets in the boat and the winds calm down, the story tells us the following: "When they had crossed over, they came to land at Gennesaret and moored the boat." (6:53). Interestingly enough, Gennesaret is on the western shore of the Sea of Galilee, which is where they were before they left! After struggling all night rowing against the wind for nine to twelve hours, they ended up just about back where they started.

We tend to miss all of this symbolism because we are not familiar with the area around the Sea of Galilee. However, audiences familiar with the region would certainly catch the irony in the apostles' destination. Is the author trying to give us historical information about location? Perhaps. But more important, the author is using references to location in order to communicate some very important truths: the twelve apostles

> A young boy had just gotten his driving permit. He asked his father if they could discuss his use of the family car. His father said, "I'll make a deal with you. You bring your grades up, study the Bible, get your hair cut, and then we'll talk about it." A month later, the boy again asked his father about using the car. The father said "Son, I'm very proud of you. You've brought your grades up, you've studied the Bible diligently, but you didn't get your hair cut." The young man waited a moment and then replied, "You know, Dad, I've been thinking about that. You know Samson had long hair, Moses had long hair, Noah had long hair, and even Jesus had long hair." His dad said, "Yes, and everywhere they went, they walked."

(the Church) had a difficult time carrying the gospel across the lake to unfamiliar territory. They could make no headway in the face of turbulence. Only Jesus can rise above this (walking on the water). Jesus alone leads them on to Tyre and Sidon and the district of the ten cities, all Gentile areas where, interestingly enough, in chapter 8 of Mark's Gospel, he again feeds a huge crowd—this time four thousand people—after they had been with him three days. All of these references to location reinforce the powerful messages in these stories—all of which are true.

"But I Need to Have Proof!"

Once, when I was delivering a Bible workshop to a group of young adults in a Chicago suburb, I covered the above examples of figurative language in the Bible and the difference between truth and fact. While the participants listened intently and accepted the approach I was taking, two main concerns surfaced. One was, "If the Bible is not all fact and uses figurative language and stories, that opens the door for anyone to interpret them any way they so desire!" Indeed, we are called upon to interpret the Bible in light of our experiences. However, we do so within a faith community and within the broader tradition of interpretation going back over two thousand years. This tradition of interpretation invites us to consider the original context in which a passage was written as well as the original author's intent. We simply cannot understand the full meaning of a Bible passage for ourselves today until we have some insight into its meaning as originally intended. It is also important to remember that while the Bible speaks to us personally it does not speak to us exclusively. We are not free to interpret the Bible any old way we please, but within the context of our Catholic Christian tradition. Our interpretation of the Bible must be done in communion with our present-day brothers and sisters in the Church as well as with those who have gone before us marked with the sign of faith.

> "Comfort in tribulation can be secured only on the sure ground of faith holding as true the words of Scripture and the teaching of the Catholic Church."
> —St. Thomas More

The second concern was even more pointed. One participant applied all of this discussion of figurative language to the story of the Resurrection and said, "I understand how this might apply to Noah's ark or some other ancient story, but I have to know that Jesus literally rose from the dead. I need proof of that!" I responded first by stating emphatically that we do know for a fact that Jesus was a historical person. Then, I stated that, without a doubt, I believe that Jesus is risen. Yet, that absolute confidence is based on testimony, not proof. No one can offer proof of the Resurrection. Not even the Bible offers proof. What we do have are the astonishing accounts of those who proclaim that their lives were completely

> **The Bible provides us with the compelling testimony of those who have encountered the risen Christ and been transformed, and who now invite us to enter into his Paschal Mystery.**

transformed by an encounter with the one they recognized as the risen Jesus. Their stories are overwhelmingly compelling—compelling enough to change the lives of millions of people over the last two thousand years.

The Resurrection is something we believe in by faith, based on powerful evidence and testimony of witnesses. Such evidence, however, falls short of proof. Each time we celebrate the Eucharist, we say, "Let us proclaim the *mystery* of our faith: Lord, by your cross and Resurrection you have set us free!" Ultimately, the Bible does not provide us with proof of anything. And yet, we can read it with absolute confidence, knowing that we can trust God, who is good to his word. The Bible provides us with the compelling testimony of those who have encountered the risen Christ and been transformed, and who now invite us to enter into his Paschal Mystery. In his book *Against an Infinite Horizon*, Ronald Rolheiser explains that "Certitude is not the real substance of faith. Faith is a way of seeing things" (9). Ultimately, Scripture helps us to see our lives, not in isolation, but against the "backdrop" of Jesus' Paschal Mystery. Robert Ludwig describes in his book *Reconstructing Catholicism: For a New Generation* how the Bible (the Gospels in particular) does this.

WATERTON FIRE DEPARTMENT

WATERTON FIRE DEPARTMENT

"Bert is inspired by the story of Pentecost, but those tongues of flame sound like a real fire hazard."

Do the Math—Numbers in the Bible

"It is our story, it is the story of all the earth, a universal story about gracious mystery as our source and destiny and the need to live by courage and trust. Yet, this story is not an 'answer' to our questions, as the fundamentalists would have it. Rather, the Gospel is the thematization of our experience of mystery, helping us make peace with our deepest questions by our acceptance of incompleteness, vulnerability, emptiness" (97).

Finally, it is important here to lend credibility to this whole discussion about the difference between truth and fact. In other words, the approach to Scripture described in this chapter is not something that I made up. Rather, it is a summary of the official position of the Catholic Church as expressed by the Pontifical Biblical Commission's document entitled, "The Interpretation of the Bible in the Church." Here are a few quotations from that document (section I. F.) that serve as the foundation for this chapter.

> Fundamentalism also places undue stress upon the inerrancy of certain details in the biblical texts, especially in what concerns historical events or supposedly scientific truth. It often historicizes material which from the start never claimed to be historical. It considers historical everything that is reported or recounted with verbs in the past tense, failing to take the necessary account of the possibility of symbolic or figurative meaning.

> It is not sufficient to translate a text word for word in order to obtain its literal sense. One must understand the text according to the literary conventions of the time. When a text is metaphorical, its literal sense is not that which flows immediately from a word-to-word translation (e.g. "Let your loins be girt": Lk 12:35), but that which corresponds to the metaphorical use of these terms ("Be ready for action"). When it is a question of a story, the literal sense does not necessarily imply belief that the facts recounted actually took place, for a story need not belong to the genre of history but be instead a work of imaginative fiction.

[Fundamentalism] refuses to admit that the inspired word of God has been expressed in human language and that this word has been expressed, under divine inspiration, by human authors possessed of limited capacities and resources. For this reason, it tends to treat the biblical text as if it had been dictated word for word by the Spirit. It fails to recognize that the word of God has been formulated in language and expression conditioned by various periods.

The fundamentalist approach is dangerous, for it is attractive to people who look to the Bible for ready answers to the problems of life. It can deceive these people, offering them interpretations that are pious but illusory, instead of telling them that the Bible does not necessarily contain an immediate answer to each and every problem. Without saying as much in so many words, fundamentalism actually invites people to a kind of intellectual suicide. It injects into life a false certitude, for it unwittingly confuses the divine substance of the biblical message with what are in fact its human limitations.

Fundamentalism is right to insist on the divine inspiration of the Bible, the inerrancy of the word of God and other biblical truths included in its five fundamental points. But its way of presenting these truths is rooted in an ideology which is not biblical, whatever the proponents of this approach might say. For it demands an unshakable adherence to rigid doctrinal points of view and imposes, as the only source of teaching for Christian life and salvation, a reading of the Bible which rejects all questioning and any kind of critical research.

It does not follow from this [text] that we can attribute to a biblical text whatever meaning we like, interpreting it in a wholly subjective way. On the contrary, one must reject as unauthentic every interpretation alien to the meaning expressed by the human authors in their written text.

In its attachment to the principle "Scripture alone," fundamentalism separates the interpretation of the Bible from the tradition, which, guided by the Spirit, has authentically developed in union with Scripture in the heart of the community of faith . . . . It presents itself as a form of private interpretation which does not acknowledge that the Church is founded on the Bible and draws its life and inspiration from Scripture.

Questions for Reflection and Discussion

- How are numbers and locations used for effect in Bible stories? What are some examples?

- What does the Pontifical Biblical Commission teach us about understanding the Bible in "The Interpretation of the Bible in the Church"? How do you feel about the approach to understanding the Bible proposed by this chapter and this document? How does this approach change your understanding of the Bible? How does it help? How does it challenge?

- What experience(s) have you had with fundamentalists or fundamentalism?

- In your own words, how would you explain the Catholic approach to understanding the Bible with regards to fundamentalism?

- Why is fundamentalism considered "dangerous" by the Pontifical Biblical Commission?

Chapter Eight

Draftsman Tools:
The Tools of Interpretation

Sketching, in general, simply involves a pen or pencil, and paper. Technical sketching, such as drafting blueprints, however, requires specialized instruments including compasses, ruling pens, protractors, and triangles—just to name a few. When it comes to reading and interpreting the Bible, we need a few tools of our own in order to better understand what God's Word is saying to us.

In Polish culture, it is customary to say, *Smacznego!* (smoch-NEH-go), when about to eat a meal with others. What does it mean in English? It's the equivalent of *Bon appétit!* Oops. Wait. That's French. So, just what does smacznego mean? Well, that's the problem. Unfortunately, the English language doesn't really have a word that exactly captures the essence of smacznego. In other words, if you ask several different people what smacznego means in English, you may get several different answers depending upon one's interpretation. When we go from one language to another, we need to interpret what we believe the original language is attempting to say.

What does this have to do with the Bible? Well, first and foremost, the Bible was *not* written in English (nor did Jesus speak English). When people get nervous about interpreting the Bible, they have to realize that every Bible that is not written in the original language of the author *is* an interpretation. Most biblical texts were originally

> But the task of authentically interpreting the word of God, whether written or handed on, has been entrusted exclusively to the living teaching office of the Church, whose authority is exercised in the name of Jesus Christ. (*Dei Verbum*, 10)

written in Hebrew or Greek. By the third century, the Old Testament books originally written in Hebrew were translated into Greek, and by the fifth century, the entire Bible was translated into Latin. As centuries progressed, the Bible was translated into dozens of languages. In other words, when someone gets upset about *contemporary* translations of the Bible, insisting that we use the *original* text (usually meaning the King James Version), they had better be prepared to read either Hebrew or Greek because there is no such thing as the *original* English text.

The Protestant Old Testament excludes the following books: Tobit, Judith, Wisdom, Sirach (Ecclesiasticus), Baruch, and First and Second Maccabees.

Every Bible is an interpretation of the original text. Therefore, we need not be afraid of the word *interpretation* when it comes to the Bible. We are called to interpret the Bible within the context of our faith tradition and within the context of the author's original intent as best we can through scholarly research. Let's take a closer look at how we interpret the Bible as a faith community and as an individual within that faith community.

How Do I Choose a Bible?

If different Bibles employ different interpretations, how can one select a Bible that is consistent with a Catholic approach to the Word of God? First, we need to understand the difference between Catholic and Protestant Bibles. While both are the inspired Word of God, it is important to note that our two traditions have different "floor plans" for organizing God's Library. Both the Catholic and Protestant traditions have developed their own final list of which books are considered inspired and thus to be included in the Bible. This final official list is referred to as the canon. The Catholic canon contains the seventy-three books we outlined earlier: forty-six Old Testament and twenty-seven New Testament. The Protestant canon includes sixty-six books, excluding seven Old Testament books: Tobit, Judith, Wisdom, Sirach (Ecclesiasticus), Baruch, and First and Second Maccabees. Why the difference?

In the first century after Christ, rabbis in Palestine gathered to form the canon of the Hebrew Scriptures. They selected only those thirty-nine books that were written in Hebrew and had existed for what they considered to be a significant period of time. Around the same time, however,

Greek-speaking Jews were using an Old Testament canon made up of forty-six books, including some books that were written in Greek or were of a more recent authorship than those in the Hebrew canon. Early Christians used both the Hebrew canon and the Greek canon of the

"It's not the most accurate or inspiring version, but my brother-in-law, Bubba, was on the translation committee."

Old Testament. Although the early Church included these seven books as part of the canon, opinion was divided regarding their canonical status. St. Jerome, who translated the Bible into Latin in the fifth century (his translation is called the Vulgate), referred to these seven books as the apocrypha, meaning "hidden." Although he included these books in his translation, he considered them to be outside of the canon. Thus, for many centuries, the exact standing of these seven Old Testament books continued to be called into question by some.

> "It is not hard for any man, who hath a Bible in his hands, to borrow good words and holy sayings in abundance; but to make them his own, is a work of grace, only from above."
> —JOHN MILTON

During the Reformation in the sixteenth century, Protestants established a canon of thirty-nine Old Testament books, using only those books recognized as canonical by the first century Jews and dismissing the apocryphal books. From this came the King James Version, which remained the standard biblical text in English until the twentieth century. Meanwhile, the Catholic Church at the Council of Trent (1545–63) definitively affirmed these seven apocryphal books as part of the canon, referring to them as deuterocanonical, which means a "second canon." Thus, the deuterocanonical books are those whose Scriptural character, once contested, have been affirmed as part of the canon of the Bible.

A Catholic Bible

Just because a Bible has the word *Catholic* on it (such as the New Living Translation: Catholic Reference Edition, by Tyndale House) does not mean that it has been approved for Catholic audiences. The best way to determine if a Bible is approved for Catholic readership is to look for what is called an imprimatur (im-pri-MAH-tur) near the inside cover of a Bible. The imprimatur, followed by the name of the Roman Catholic authority issuing it, indicates that the translation is acceptable for use by Roman Catholics.

So, the first thing to know about the differences between Catholic and Protestant Bibles is in terms of which books are included. However, using this rule on its own can be tricky because many Protestant publishers, eager to get a share in the growing market for Catholic Bible readership, are now including the deuterocanonical books in their Bible editions. This leads us to a second way the two types of Bible versions differ—in the content of the support materials, study helps, and learning tools, such as footnotes and commentaries. When these support materials venture into the area of doctrine, the differences between a Catholic Bible and a Protestant Bible can be profound. For example, support materials in a Protestant Bible may make reference to the recognition of two—and only two—sacraments: Baptism and the Lord's Supper. Catholics, of course, recognize seven sacraments. Some Protestant Bibles include support materials that take a fundamentalist approach not in keeping with the Catholic approach we covered in the last chapter. Finally, a few Protestant Bibles (e.g., the Scofield Bible, the Tyndale Bible) can include support materials that are blatantly anti-Catholic. So, if you are seeking an interpretation of biblical texts that is in line with Catholic Tradition, it is best to use a Catholic Bible.

Well into the twentieth century, the only Catholic versions of the Bible were translated from St. Jerome's Latin version of the fifth century. In 1943, Pope Pius XII called for a Catholic translation based on the earliest available manuscripts and the original languages. Since that time, several translations have been made under Catholic sponsorship.

Which translation do we use at Mass on Sundays? The New American Bible (NAB) is the translation that we hear proclaimed at Mass in the United States. It makes sense to use this translation in your own studies and prayer since it will be reinforced at Sunday liturgy. A very popular version of the New American Bible is the Catholic Study Bible, which provides extensive footnotes and commentary. Another very popular Catholic Bible is the New Jerusalem Bible (NJB). The NJB was translated primarily by Catholic scholars in Great Britain. Another version that is more ecumenical in the makeup of its Scripture scholars but still carries an imprimatur is the New Revised Standard Version (NRSV). Rather than attempting to provide an exhaustive guide to selecting Bibles, know that if a Bible carries an imprimatur, it is considered acceptable for Catholic readership.

The Apocryphal Gospels

Some books, such as the Gospel of Thomas or the Gospel of Mary Magdalene, didn't make it into the Bible. Such writings that have not been included in the New Testament are referred to as *apocryphal*, meaning "hidden" or "secret." From the beginning of the Church, the faithful did not embrace these books as inspired Scripture. While Biblical scholars believe that some of these writings may include actual words and events from Jesus' life (most of which have parallels in the four Gospels of the New Testament), most lack real historical value and even include outlandish accounts of Jesus' life that attempt to fill in the cracks supposedly left by the other Gospels. On the other hand, it is from these apocryphal accounts that we get the names of Mary's parents, Joachim and Anne, and the legend of the blossoming of Joseph's staff as a sign that he was to take Mary as his bride. In other words, the apocryphal Gospels are valuable pieces of literature but are not considered inspired Scripture.

Recognizing Different Types of Literature

No doubt, you do not read all of your mail in the same manner. Junk mail gets tossed with nary a glance while personal mail may be read over and over (and kept under your pillow at night!) The more mail you get (and the older and wiser you become), the better you become at identifying what type of mail it is you are about to read. You even learn not to be fooled by the envelopes that tell you you may have just won ten million dollars.

One of the first steps involved in interpreting the Bible is to learn to identify just what type of literature it is that you are reading. Like sorting out the daily mail, you can separate different types of biblical literature into different categories. Just as we do not read all of our mail in the same way, we do not read every type of biblical literature in the same manner.

The more we read the Bible, the better we will become at differentiating a parable from a proverb, a genealogy from a discourse, a psalm from a letter, and a prophecy from a legal code.

The key to determining what type of literature you are reading in the Bible is to look at what you're reading within its broader context. Each book of the Bible has its own introduction that will often tell you what type of literature you are about to encounter. Likewise, the footnotes we discussed earlier will often reveal clues about the type of literature under scrutiny. Finally, any Scripture passage must be interpreted in light of its broader context, namely, in relation to the preceding and following chapters and verses.

Let's take a look at an example. Suppose we were reading the following passage:

> As in all the churches of the saints, women should be silent in the churches. For they are not permitted to speak, but should be subordinate, as the law also says. If there is anything they desire to know, let them ask their husbands at home. For it is shameful for a woman to speak in church. (1 Cor 14:33–35)

The coordinator of the parish Bible study decided to invite his new neighbor to attend the next session. He knocked on the door and thought he could hear someone moving about, but his repeated knocks went unanswered. He took out a business card and wrote "Revelation 3:20" ("Listen! I am standing at the door, knocking") on the back of it and stuck it in the door. The next morning, he found that his card had been returned to his own doorstep. On the back was written, "Genesis 3:10." Reaching for his Bible to check out the citation, he found the following passage: "I heard the sound of you in the garden, and I was afraid, because I was naked."

What are we to make of a passage like this? If we take this passage literally and isolated from its context, we can conclude that women should not be allowed any speaking roles in our celebrations of the Eucharist. But, we know this is not true because women and men participate in all of the spoken responses of the Mass. Likewise, women may serve as lectors, proclaiming God's Word to the assembly. Let's take a look at some key questions we must ask any time we attempt to properly interpret Scripture.

Copyright © Doug Hall, 1991. Used by Permission.

"Willard, I'm starting to question your interpretation of those passages about submission."

What type of literature is this? If we go back to the title of the book that this passage is taken from, we find that we are reading from the first *letter* of Paul to the Corinthians. This means that we are reading a letter written to a specific group of people who lived in Corinth during the first century AD We need to understand the general purpose of Paul's letters and the role they played in the early Church. When we recognize this literature as a letter, we recognize that we need to get the flavor of the whole letter before we isolate specific verses.

What do we know of the author? In many books of the Bible, we do not know precisely who the author was. In this passage, we are fortunate enough to know that St. Paul is the writer. The more we know about St. Paul's style of writing and his theology, the better we are able to interpret passages from his work. Paul was not afraid to speak his mind and felt very strongly about the need for order in the community.

Who was the target audience for this work? Who were the people of Corinth? In order to understand this passage, we need to learn a little bit about the people it was addressed to. Depending on the Bible version you are using, there may be some good background information on audience in the introduction to 1 Corinthians. In this example, we discover that the Church of Corinth had many problems. Paul felt it was his responsibility to address these problems in a straightforward manner to achieve order in the community.

What is the overall thrust of the chapter of the book? Taken in isolation, we can conclude that this passage compels us to forbid women to speak in church. However, when we look at the overall context of Paul's first letter to the Corinthians, we find that Paul seems to be contradicting some earlier statements he made about the role of women at worship. In chapter 11, verse 5, Paul writes that "any woman who prays or prophesies with her head unveiled disgraces her head." Here, Paul clearly is addressing the possibility of women speaking in liturgical leadership roles. When we return to 14:34–35, we find upon close examination that Paul is referring to the notion of women *asking questions* during the liturgy ("If there is anything they desire to know, let them ask their husbands at home"). He is not suggesting here that women have no role in worship. He is talking about keeping order in the assembly. In fact, the overall context of this chapter and the whole book reveals that Paul is trying to establish liturgical order and reconcile differing factions. So, taken in context, Paul is not so much speaking about the role of women as he is speaking about liturgical order and about ending the chaos and confusion that reigned at Corinthian liturgical assemblies.

> **The more we read the Bible, the better we will become at differentiating a parable from a proverb, a genealogy from a discourse, a psalm from a letter, and a prophecy from a legal code.**

How do we interpret this passage for today? It is our responsibility as individuals within a faith tradition to interpret what this passage is saying to us today. Paul was speaking to a culture in which the role of women was profoundly different than it is in most cultures and societies today. His comments on women are the result of the culture in which he was writing. Today, we must ask what the proper liturgical roles are when we gather to celebrate Eucharist; what our present-day understanding of the equality and dignity of women is; and how the words of St. Paul can inspire us to celebrate liturgy with proper respect for its rubrics, roles, and order.

Interpretation Tools: Forms of Criticism

It is through the process of interpretation that the Word of God continues to speak to people throughout the ages. The Bible was written at a time when most people were farmers or at least intimately familiar with rural life and lived under monarchic rule. When the biblical authors recorded their experiences of God's saving presence in their lives, they did not have a society of cellular phones, Internet-wired personal computers, and laser technology. For that reason, it is up to us, with the guidance of the Holy Spirit and the Church, to interpret the Word of God as it applies to our contemporary situation. Despite the new world we live in, the central experiences of life remain unaltered. The Word of God is timeless. We need only to transport it from its original setting and language to our contemporary situation. In order to do this, Scripture scholars offer us some very helpful tools for interpretation called forms of criticism. Let's take a brief look at some.

The Word of God is timeless.

Historical Criticism This method of criticism attempts to ascertain as accurately as possible what the author's original intent was. Historical criticism looks closely at what was happening at the time, what the people of the time were experiencing, and the audience for whom the author was writing. Today, archeology plays an important role in learning as much as we can about the place and times of the Scripture passage in question. Another aspect of the historical approach is the attempt to determine who the author actually was. We know today that it was common practice in biblical times to credit a literary work to someone who may not have actually taken pen to paper. Today, we consider that fraud. Recall, however, that the Bible was recorded in a time when most people were illiterate. Most forms of literature were passed along orally for decades, if not centuries, before they were written down. As with any oral tradition, the stories take on the flavor of those passing them along. Since we believe that the Bible is the inspired Word of God, we are saying that God inspired this entire process. In the end, as long as a piece of literature was said to have been from the tradition of an individual, it was deemed proper to add that person's name to the title of the book. This does not take away from the validity of the Bible but reveals how God works through a very human process to shape the Word into flesh. The better we understand this whole process, the closer we can come to the original intent of the work before we attempt to apply it to our own lives.

Textual Criticism When discussing Scripture, we will sometimes hear people say, "If we go back to the *original* text . . ." It sounds good. All we need to do is go back to the original text and see exactly what was written, translate it as closely as possible into English, and we'll know exactly what the text says.

There's only one problem. We have no original texts. We do not have any of the Psalms written in David's own handwriting on parchment. We have none of Paul's letters on the original stationery. All we have are early manuscripts, which are the earliest known *copies* of all the works of the Bible. When Scripture scholars go back to the original text, then, they are going back to the earliest available copies. Textual criticism attempts to look at these early manuscripts, many of which contain inconsistencies among the different copies, and try to determine what they said in their original language so that the best interpretation can be made when translation is attempted.

New approaches to textual criticism

CRUMMY TYPE!

CHEAP PAPER!

LOUSY PUNCTUATION!

Copyright © Doug Hall, 1991. Used by Permission.

Form Criticism With Paul's letter to the Corinthians, we talked about how important it is to know what type of literature you are reading. Form criticism attempts to determine precisely what type of literature we are dealing with, how that form of literature was understood in its time, and how we are to understand it today. We all recognize that different forms of literature are appropriate for different occasions. For example, we may encounter many forms of literature that are associated with someone dying.

- a death certificate
- a last will and testament
- an obituary
- a eulogy
- stories
- a homily

All of these forms of literature have a unique purpose and a proper place when one says goodbye to a loved one. Some are legal documents. Some are informal anecdotes. Some are ritual expressions. We know how to sort these out and put them in their proper

Oldest Biblical Manuscripts

Some of the oldest known Old Testament manuscripts are fragments of the Dead Sea Scrolls, discovered in 1947 at Qumran. Some of these fragments date between 150 BC to AD 70. The oldest known manuscript fragments of the New Testament date from the late first century to the early second century. The oldest full manuscripts of the New Testament are dated from the fourth century.

place, and we know how to interpret them. Form criticism attempts to do the same. It is a way of sorting out what we are reading in the Bible and determining how to best interpret it given its literary form.

Source Criticism Today, it is considered plagiarism to use someone else's idea in your own writing without giving him or her proper credit. In biblical times, this was not the case. It was common practice for one author to use other sources and edit, delete, incorporate, or expand upon them. Source criticism attempts to determine what previous sources an author may have had at his fingertips and how that source may have influenced the piece we are reading. Here's an example that works a bit like a word problem or a brain teaser:

- The Gospel of Matthew has more than 600 verses in it that appear in Mark's Gospel (which most scholars believe was written first).
- The Gospel of Luke, also written after Mark, contains more than 300 verses of Mark's Gospel.
- It seems clear that Matthew and Luke relied heavily upon Mark's Gospel to write their own.

- Strangely enough, however, Matthew and Luke have 240 verses in common that are *not* from Mark.

- Matthew and Luke were not written at the same time, in the same place, or by the same author.

- How can they share 240 verses in common that cannot be traced to another earlier-known Gospel?

This mystery suggests to Scripture scholars that both Matthew and Luke had a source other than Mark upon which they relied to write their Gospels. Unfortunately, we do not know what this source was. Scripture scholars refer to this mysterious source simply as Q, the first letter of the German word *quelle* that means "source." Source criticism, then, attempts to look at the sources available to biblical authors and how these may have influenced later versions.

Redaction Criticism Take a look at the end of Mark's Gospel. Note that it has four endings.

- The story seems to end at Mk 16:8 when the women leave the tomb in great fear and say nothing to anyone.

- Next, we encounter something called the "Longer Ending," from Mk 16:9–20, that includes Jesus appearing to the disciples and ascending to Heaven.

- Following this, we encounter something called the "Shorter Ending," which captures the essence of the "Longer Ending" in just a couple of sentences.

- Finally, we come upon something called the "Freer Logion," which may be in a footnote. This ending attempts to explain why the disciples were so hesitant to believe that Jesus had risen.

If you read your footnotes and commentaries about these passages, you will learn that various early copies of Mark's Gospel end differently. These various endings appear to be attempts by editors to provide a more satisfying ending than Mark originally did in 16:8. Redaction criticism attempts to discover what portions of Scripture may have been altered or affected by later editors and why. These alterations should not be viewed suspiciously, nor should they in any way taint our understanding of the validity of the Scripture we are reading. Rather, they provide for us a window into the minds of people who were attempting to do just what we are trying to do: discover a way of making God's Word speak to the present age. Their interpretation serves to inspire us to interpret the Bible for our own experience.

All of these forms of biblical criticism are not meant to strip the Bible of its power and mystery but open it up to us. We ourselves may not have conducted the actual scholarly studies and criticisms, but we should use the discoveries made by Scripture scholars to open our eyes to the richness of God's Word and enhance our understanding of the Bible.

Questions for Reflection and Discussion

- How would you explain or characterize the differences between Protestant and Catholic Bibles?

- What does it mean to interpret the Bible?

- What do we need in order to safeguard against interpreting the Bible recklessly?

- What are some of the different types of literature you are familiar with in the Bible?

- What are some of the different forms of criticism used by Scripture scholars to guide us in our interpretation of Scripture? Describe them in your own words.

- Which form of biblical criticism do you find most fascinating? Why?

Chapter Nine

First Steps and Next Steps

If you want to learn how to read blueprints, you can go online and find lots of places to begin. You can also attend seminars that will take you further. If you're really serious, you can take college courses and perhaps eventually end up with a degree in architecture. When it comes to reading the Bible, it's good to know where to begin and what some of the next steps are. This book is only the beginning.

Now that you've chosen your translation of the Bible and you're equipped with the knowledge and skills needed to read, study, and interpret the Scriptures, you may be wondering one more thing: where do I begin? If the Bible can indeed be compared to a library, then allow me to act as reference librarian for a moment and recommend some starting points.

The Old Testament

The first twenty chapters of the book of Exodus The Exodus story is the centerpiece of the entire Old Testament—the defining moment of the people of Israel, you might say. Besides, you can't go wrong with all of the drama and theatrics of burning bushes, deadly plagues, and parting seas.

The book of Psalms The Bible is intended to deepen our faith and our prayer life. What better place to begin than with an entire book of prayers? The Psalms will provide you with easy reading and profound inspiration for every mood and occasion.

The synod recommends the formation of small ecclesial communities where the Word of God is heard, studied, and prayed. ("Word of God in the Life and Mission of the Church," Synod of Bishops, October 2008, Proposition 21)

The book of Proverbs If you are looking for wisdom, this is a good place to start. Reading Proverbs is like sitting down with your grandparents to get all of the profound insights they have collected through their years of experience. Many people begin and/or end their day with a passage from Proverbs.

The New Testament

The Acts of the Apostles Acts is a good place to start because it is the story that most closely resembles our own experience—followers of Jesus struggling to preach the gospel after his ascension into Heaven.

The Gospel of Mark If you want to get into the Gospels right away, begin with Mark. Mark's Gospel is the shortest and easiest to read. His "just the facts" approach allows you to cover the whole Gospel story in just a few hours, something that is highly recommended.

Tips for Reading and Praying the Bible

Typically, when you read a book, you just pick it up and jump right in. Reading the Bible is different. In essence, we do not *read* the Bible, we *pray* the Bible. Once you know what passage you are going to read (keep it short; don't try to take on too much), follow these simple steps:

1. Set a prayerful mood of quiet.
2. Pray to the Holy Spirit to open up your mind and heart to the Word of God.
3. Read the passage once slowly. Look over any footnotes and commentary that will assist your understanding of the passage.
4. Go back and read the passage again, this time more slowly and prayerfully. If the passage describes a story or event, use your imagination to place yourself within the scene as a participant. Pause at phrases, words, or images that speak to you and allow them to resonate. Whereas your first read-through is for the head, this one is for the heart.
5. Be quiet. Let the Word of God continue to echo in your heart, mind, and soul.
6. Pray in your own words thanking God for the Word and asking for the grace you need to apply (interpret) it to your life.

The Letter of Paul to the Philippians Sit back and imagine that Paul is writing to you personally. This letter is inspirational and contains one of the most powerful and well-known Christian passages: Phil 2:5–11.

Lectio Divina

One form of praying with Scripture that Catholics have used for centuries is called *lectio divina* (LECT-see-oh dih-VEE-nah), Latin for "sacred reading." This is a way of spending time with the Word of God using a special form of reading and listening so that you can hear God "with the ear of your heart" (St. Benedict, *The Rule of St. Benedict*). This form of prayer follows four steps.

1. *Lectio* (reading)—slowly and prayerfully read aloud a brief Scripture passage, repeating the passage up to three times after a silent pause between each reading. Allow a word or phrase to speak to you in a special way.

2. *Meditatio* (meditation)—silently reflect, for a few minutes, upon the word or phrase that is speaking to you. In doing so, take the word or phrase to heart and allow it to interact with your own thoughts, hopes, desires, and memories.

3. *Oratio* (prayer)—enter into a silent dialogue with God for a few minutes, speaking as one friend speaks to another and allowing yourself to be touched and changed by God's Word.

4. *Contemplatio* (contemplation)—simply rest silently and prayerfully in God's embrace for a few minutes. By letting go of your own words, allow the Word of God to speak to your heart in silence.

For resources on *lectio divina*, see the Annotated Bibliography for Catholic Scripture Study on page 114 of the Bible Resources section of this book.

This Is *My* Story—This Is *Our* Story

The refrain to the wonderful Christian hymn "Blessed Assurance" shouts, "This is my story." We should sing this refrain every time we pick up the Bible. Certainly, the Bible is full of stories about people who lived several thousand years ago in a land far, far away from most of us. Ultimately, however, these Bible stories are somehow the story of your life and my life and the life of the Christian community. The reason these Bible stories are considered sacred and inspired is because, throughout the ages, they have been seen as the stories that capture and express the experience of salvation for all people for all time. In other words, the Bible is about living now and forever—it is a living Word!

As we read and pray the Bible, the ultimate act of interpretation is when we ask the question, "How is this *my* story?" Unless we take this step, the Bible will remain something impersonal and remote. When we ask this question, we open up a whole new relationship in our lives. Now, God is no longer just speaking to Moses, Abraham and Sarah, Jeremiah, Jonah, Peter, Zacchaeus, the woman at the well, Martha and Mary, and Paul. When we read the Bible—Paul's letters, Jesus' words to the apostles—we are hearing God speaking to us.

How do we make this happen? How do we make the Bible stories our own? We need to follow two simple steps:

1. First and foremost, we must ask what the text is actually saying and to whom it was originally addressed. Before applying the Bible to our own lives, it can be beneficial to understand the lives of the people who are involved in the story.

2. Second, once we have made an effort to understand the original intent of the author and the experience of the original audience, we must ask "How is this story about me?" and "How is this story about the community of faith?"

When we do this, we realize that

- The Exodus event was not just about the journey of the people of Israel from slavery in Egypt to freedom in the Promised Land; it is the story of our own personal journey from the slavery of sin to the freedom we find in the place where we encounter God.

- The story of Jonah and the large fish is not just about a cowardly man turned prophet; it is the story of what happens to us whenever we try to run from the will of God—we find that God cannot be outrun.

- The stories of Jesus healing the blind, deaf, paralyzed, and unclean are not just tales of wonder from long ago; they are stories of how Jesus has the power to heal us when we cannot see, when our ears are closed, when we are stained by sin, and when we are paralyzed by fear, greed, or anger. The song "Amazing Grace" personalizes the experience by proclaiming, "I once was lost, but now am found, was blind, but now I see."

"I'm interested in relating our Bible study to topics of current concern, like gas mileage."

- The story of Jesus appearing to the two disciples on the road to Emmaus is no longer just a mysterious story of two disciples who could not recognize Jesus; it becomes the story of how we seem to be unable to recognize the risen Christ in our midst until we listen to his Word and break bread. In fact, this story contains a clue as to how we must insert ourselves into Scripture stories. Only one of the two disciples in the story is named: Cleopas. The other disciple remains unnamed. The author of this story seems to have done this on purpose in order to entice each one of us to insert ourselves into the story. *We* are the other disciple. *We* are often directionless. *We* have experienced pain and loss. *We* are unable to recognize the presence of Jesus even though he walks with us. It is through the reading and study of Scripture that we, like the two disciples on the road to Emmaus, develop a desire to gather around the table and break bread. When we do this, our eyes are opened and we recognize the presence of the risen Lord in our midst.

In brief, the story of the woman at the well is the story of how we thirst. The story of the man born blind is the story of how we need to see with Jesus' eyes. The story of the raising of Lazarus is the story of how each of us is dead, wrapped up, and buried, and in need of being called forth to new life. The story of the Passion, death, and Resurrection of Jesus is the story of how we come to be born again only by dying to our old selves. The story of Pentecost is the story of how we are gifted and sent forth by the Spirit to proclaim this Good News to others.

Now Is the Acceptable Time

During one of my Bible presentations to a group of Catholic young adults, one participant admitted that she had only recently begun to learn about the Bible by attending Scripture study. She was excited about the new knowledge and nourishment that she was receiving. I asked her if she was attending this

"Edward is interested in Bible study, and I'm interested in fellowship."

Scripture study at a Catholic church or a Protestant church. She turned red and sheepishly admitted that she was attending a Protestant Bible study. Not wanting to discourage her in any way or proliferate any form of anti-Protestant suspicion, I affirmed her zeal. I commented that while I would prefer that she attend a Catholic Bible study, if none were being offered, it was good that she was being nourished by the Word of God from our Protestant brothers and sisters. Before I could move on, another participant strongly objected, not out of any distrust of Protestants, but out of a sense of shame that no Catholic churches in the area were offering Bible study. He said, "If there are no Bible studies in any of the area Catholic churches, then, by God, we had better start one . . . now!" During the break, I observed as several participants surrounded the pastor eagerly offering to help set up a Bible study program for the parish. (See the Bible Resources, page 104, for suggestions on how to do this.)

I couldn't agree more with the young man's comments. The time has come for Catholics to take ownership of the Bible. To loosely quote St. Paul in his second letter to the Corinthians, "NOW is the acceptable time!" (6:2). As St. Jerome once said, "Ignorance of the Scriptures is ignorance of Christ" (*Dei Verbum*, 25). The Second Vatican Council stated firmly that "Access to Sacred Scripture ought to be open wide to the Christian faithful." (*Catechism of the Catholic Church*, 131). The time has come for us Catholics to embrace, with enthusiastic zeal and profound openness, the gift of God's Word given to us in holy Scripture. When it comes to our approach to the Bible, we should heed the words of Deuteronomy: "Keep these words that I am commanding you today in your heart. Recite them to your children and talk about them when you are at home and when you are away, when you lie down and when you rise. Bind them as a sign on your hand, fix them as an emblem on your forehead, and write them on the doorposts of your house and on your gates" (6:6–9). Or, to put it in a form more familiar to Catholics (as we sign our forehead, lips, and breast before the Gospel each week at Mass): "May the Word of God be in our minds, on our lips, and in our hearts."

A pastor who was coordinating Bible study was giving the group an assignment for the next session. "Next week," he said, "we are going to explore the virtues of truth and honesty. In preparation for our session, I want you all to read the seventeenth chapter of Mark." The following week, at the beginning of the Bible study, the pastor said, "Now then, all of you who have prepared for the lesson by reading the seventeenth chapter of Mark, please step to the front of the room." About half the group rose and came forward. "The rest of you may leave," said the pastor, "these folks are the ones I obviously need to talk to about truth and honesty. There is no seventeenth chapter in the Gospel of Mark."

Questions for Reflection and Discussion

- What does it mean that every Bible story is somehow your story?

- Have you had any experience with Bible study? If so, describe it. If not, would you consider participating in a Catholic Bible study? Why or why not?

- How might your relationship to the Bible change as a result of reading this book?

- What will you do to deepen your knowledge of the Bible? What is the next best step for you?

BIBLE RESOURCES

How to Begin a Bible Program in Your Parish

The most important resources for beginning a Bible program in your parish are, first, people who desire to grow closer to God and, second, copies of the Bible! With these two resources serving as the foundation, your parish can begin a Bible program using a variety of resources available from many fine Catholic publishers.

Generally, there are three approaches to engaging people with the Bible. The first approach is **Bible discussion.** In this model, the goal is to give people a concentrated exposure to the scriptural texts—supported by solid scholarship—with the intention of inviting a personal response and practical application of the Scriptures to one's life. A popular example of this is Six Weeks with the Bible (Loyola Press). Bible discussion programs such as Six Weeks with the Bible are arranged in short, flexible installments that can fit easily into a parish Advent or Lenten program. At the same time, the flexibility allows for groups to stretch their discussion of a book or theme beyond the suggested time frame, depending on the needs of the group.

The second approach is **Bible study.** In this model, the goal is to deepen one's understanding of the Scripture text. Two examples of this approach are Little Rock Scripture Study (Diocese of Little Rock and Liturgical Press) and the Denver Catholic Biblical School (Diocese of Denver). Bible study programs are like a Bible course. They are typically longer than a Bible discussion program; they require homework, call for a greater commitment of participation, and need more skilled facilitation.

The third approach is **lectionary based.** In this model, participants enter into Scripture through the readings used at Sunday Mass throughout the liturgical year. A lectionary-based approach combines elements of both application and study with the additional goal of enhancing one's worship experience. A popular example of this is Celebrating the Lectionary (Liturgy Training Publications), which invites participants to study and reflect on the Sunday Scripture readings throughout the liturgical year.

Whichever model you select, here are some basic steps to follow in getting your program off the ground.

- Gather a core group of 3–4 people to meet with someone on the pastoral staff of the parish to propose a Bible program. Together, identify what it is that parishioners are looking for and explore some of the Bible programs that are available from Catholic publishers. Select a model (Bible discussion, Bible study, lectionary based) that you feel meets the needs of parishioners. Likewise, identify and agree on "ground rules," such as what degree of participation and self-revelation will be encouraged, how people will listen to one another, and how participants will maintain confidentiality.

"Wow... only eighteen weeks to go in our study of Lamentations."

- Together with someone from the pastoral staff, spend some time training two or three parishioners in the skill of facilitating. The facilitator is *not* a Scripture scholar or Bible expert, he or she is someone who is able—or can learn how—to move the process or discussion along in an orderly and effective manner.

- Survey parishioners to determine the most suitable day, time, and place for the program and coordinate logistics with the parish staff. If possible, offer the program at two different times and offer child care so that parents of young children can participate as well.

- Publicize well, not just in the parish bulletin. Request the opportunity to offer a two-minute invitation from the pulpit after communion at all the Sunday Masses and follow up with an information table at the back of the church or in the parish center over coffee and cake.

The format of the gatherings should be simple enough so that the constant presence of parish staff personnel is not required. Lack of staff presence is no reason for Catholics not to engage in a Bible program. Programs such as Six Weeks With the Bible, Little Rock Scripture Study, the Denver Catholic Biblical School, and Celebrating the Lectionary provide guidance and background in their materials so that group leadership can focus on facilitating and not necessarily on Scripture scholarship. While most Bible study and discussion programs suggest a time format to follow, here is a generalized suggested format.

1. Gather over refreshments for fifteen minutes. Be sure to select a setting that is comfortable and hospitable—avoid classroom atmospheres.

2. The facilitator should welcome all participants and ensure that everyone has a Bible. Arrange to have on hand a number of Bibles of the same translation for those who do not have one. Again, the New American Bible is the one used in the U.S. Catholic lectionary.

3. The facilitator invites participants to locate the Bible passage(s) that will be the focus of the gathering. For example, in a lectionary-based program, the facilitator indicates which Sunday of the liturgical year is upcoming and which readings will be proclaimed at Mass. Participants should locate the readings in their Bible with the assistance of the facilitator and other participants. This exercise is an important part of the study. Unless we begin to discover where these readings are in the Bible, we will continue to suffer from bibliaphobia. Avoid reading Scripture passages that are reprinted in other resources such as missalettes and workbooks—let's get those Bibles out and start using them.

4. Light a candle and put on some reflective music. Spend three to five minutes in quiet preparation to read/pray the Scripture. You may also wish to invite all to stand and join hands in a circle and invite participants to offer out loud the prayers or petitions they bring with them. The only thing that Catholics sometimes fear more than reading the Bible is the notion of praying out loud with others. This format should encourage Catholics to become more comfortable with both.

5. Often, programs will offer several general nonthreatening questions to begin discussion and lead participants to reflect on their own life

experience before moving into Scripture. Generally, spend ten to fifteen minutes on this discussion.

6. Invite one of the participants to slowly and prayerfully read the identified Scripture passage(s) while all follow along in their Bibles. If the passage is long, consider inviting participants to take turns reading sections. Pause in silence for a minute or two and then invite another participant or participants to read it again.

7. Use your selected resources to provide background, commentary, and discussion questions based on the selected Scripture passage(s). Spend some time engaging participants in discussion using the resources you've chosen. You may also wish to ask a pastoral staff member or qualified parishioner to do a brief presentation on the background or commentary. Consider audio- or videotaping the mini-lecture for future use. Programs such as Little Rock Scripture Study offer the option of purchasing audiotaped or videotaped lectures.

8. During discussion, the facilitator should be sure to invite participants to offer insights and comments they have on the Scripture passage(s) and especially ways to apply insights from Scripture to daily living. Invite any questions that participants may have. Write down questions that cannot be answered by anyone present and designate someone to research the answer with a pastoral staff member or with assistance from the diocesan office.

9. The facilitator can once again invite all to stand and join hands, inviting all present to share aloud prayers of thanksgiving. A sung refrain that can be learned and led easily may be sung as a way of giving praise as well.

10. Invite participants to remain for refreshments and invite them back again for the next session. Identify the focus of the next session as well as any homework that participants should do in preparation.

11. Be sure to continue ongoing publicity, especially inviting new parishioners and the newly initiated. Avoid the temptation to become a clique. If the size of the group is becoming too large to allow for sharing and discussion, have a plan in place to break up into smaller groups led by additional trained facilitators.

Note: Pastors and pastoral staffs are stretched thin with numerous responsibilities. The key to any Bible program format is to train parishioners to facilitate these gatherings so that they do not rely upon the presence of a staff member at all times. Such an approach allows staff members to attend occasionally or drop in regularly. Facilitator training programs are available from a variety of publishers to teach the skills of leading discussion and prayer, and handling difficult people and situations. Contact your diocesan catechetical office for assistance.

Finally, another thought to consider is the question of whether the proposed Bible program needs to be a parish program at all. Four or five couples can easily get together in their homes and do a Bible discussion without the guidance of the parish staff. With parish staffs stretched thin by the demands of their ministry, Catholics can take the initiative to pursue a deeper understanding of God's Word on their own, using the quality materials provided by Catholic publishers.

Conducting a Bible Workshop for Young People (Middle and High School Students)

This workshop can be accomplished in ninety minutes and requires one adult for every twelve to fifteen children. It may also be adapted for teens and adults. The workshop requires that all participants have the same version of a Catholic Bible on hand so that page numbers can be used to locate passages quickly. It also requires that each participant have a set of the Bible bookmarks (see pages 125–131) and a pair of scissors.

Goal: To build participants' familiarity and comfort with the structure of the Bible and to increase the ease with which participants locate books, chapters, verses, and famous stories/figures in the Bible.

Learning Outcomes: Participants will learn to quickly locate biblical books, chapters, and verses using the table of contents. Likewise, participants will learn to quickly identify the location of famous stories and figures by using the *Bible Blueprint* bookmarks.

Action Plan:

1. Be sure all participants have the same version of a Catholic Bible, preferably the New American Bible.

2. Begin by introducing the notion of how important the Bible is to us as Christians and how we are going to learn more about the Bible in this session. Ask how many have heard of the following stories (raise hands):

   > David and Goliath
   >
   > Noah's ark
   >
   > Jonah and the large fish
   >
   > Jesus in the Garden of Gethsemane

3. Next, tell participants that you will offer a prize (e.g., $1 or $5) to the first person who can find one of these stories in the Bible in 60 seconds or less. Use a stopwatch (and a whistle) and give 60 seconds for each of

the four stories listed above, one at a time (without adult assistance). Most likely, no one will be able to do so. (If you believe your audience is more astute than this, be sure to allow only 30–45 seconds lest you go broke!)

Point out how unfortunate it is that we know about these stories but we don't know how to find them in the Bible. Explain that we will be working on that in this workshop.

Next, tell participants to have their Bible ready. Write the following biblical citations on the board (be sure to use abbreviations):

> Ez 12:6–8
> Jb 2:3–11
> 1 Thes 5:2–4

Again, allow participants 30–60 seconds to locate these passages (again, without adult assistance). Most will be unable to do so in the time allotted. Point out once again how unfortunate it is that we seem to be unable to identify Bible passages by their abbreviations. Ask if anyone can say out loud what the above abbreviations stand for.

4. Explain that if the Bible is so important to us, then we are going to need to learn how to find things in it more quickly and with more confidence. Explain that the Bible is not really a book but is a library —God's Library.

5. Explain that when you go to a library, you need to use the catalog and the book numbering system to locate the book you want to read. Point out how God's Library, the Bible, has a "catalog," too, namely, the table of contents. Have all participants open their Bible to the table of contents section at the beginning. Adult supervisors should assist children here. Point out the alphabetical index, the abbreviation page, and other highlights of the table of contents in your version of the Bible.

6. Using the table of contents, invite participants to tell you what page the following books begin on:

> Deuteronomy
> Judges
> Esther
> Luke

Next, using the abbreviation table, ask participants to identify which book you are referring to when you write on the board:

Hb

Na

Ti

7. Using the board, point out how book, chapter, and verse are used in biblical citation:

Title of Book (abbreviated) Chapter: Verse(s)

Invite several participants to go to the board with their Bible open to the abbreviation table and write out in biblical citation the following passages as you say them:

Ecclesiastes, chapter 9, verses 1–8 (Answer: Eccl 9:1–8)
Second Letter of Paul to Timothy, chapter 2, verses 4–6
(Answer: 2 Tim 2:4–6)

(Select more, if you wish, depending on the size of your crowd, how quickly they are catching on, and how much time you have left.)

Once again, Scripture citation may be handled differently than what I've shown above, depending on which Bible you are using. While most Bibles use the system I've described, don't be surprised to find that some Bibles use a period or a comma instead of a colon to indicate the difference between chapter and verse. For example, the Scripture citation for the Gospel of John, chapter 3, verse 16 may appear in any of the following ways, depending upon which Bible you are using: Jn 3:16; Jn 3, 16; or Jn 3.16. Be sure everyone is "on the same page" with your approach to Scripture citation before you move on.

8. Now, explain how to find famous stories and passages when we don't know what book, chapter, and verse they are in. Use the concept of God's Library again and draw a diagram on a chalkboard (see diagram from page 3 in chapter 1). Imagine a building divided into two parts: Old Testament and New Testament. Ask how we differentiate between these two. (Answer: The Old Testament has stories about the people of Israel before Jesus, the New Testament has stories about Jesus and the Christian Church.)

Invite all participants to locate the place in the Bible where the Old Testament ends and the New Testament begins. Show how much larger the Old Testament is than the New Testament. Ask participants what section they should be in if they are going to look for a story about Jesus.

9. Explain that in addition to breaking down the Bible into two large sections, we are now going to break it down into eight smaller sections, four in each testament. Distribute to each participant a set of Bible bookmarks (see pages 125–131) and a pair of scissors. (You may wish to have the bookmarks cut out ahead of time to avoid use of scissors and to reduce the time spent cutting.)

10. Beginning with the Old Testament, identify the four sections: Pentateuch, History, Wisdom, Prophets. Have participants cut out and place one bookmark at a time in their Bibles, beginning with Pentateuch. Explain what can be found in this section by using the information provided on the bookmark. Have participants find the first and last page of each section, list the books included in this section, and insert the bookmark at the end of the section. For example, the Pentateuch bookmark goes on the last page of Deuteronomy. Invite the participants to hold up the Pentateuch section alone (take the section between the thumb and index finger) to observe its length. Using the bookmark, point out what stories/people can be found in this section. Invite participants to locate a few. Do the same for each of the four sections of the Old Testament.

11. Do the same with each of the four sections of the New Testament: Gospels, Acts, Letters, Revelation. Point out that while Acts and Revelation are individual books and not really "sections," it is easier to separate them this way. Continue cutting out and inserting bookmarks one section at a time as you give a brief overview of what can be found in each section. Encourage participants to locate some stories as you talk about them. Spend extra time pointing out the Gospel section. Ask participants to hold up the section from Matthew through John: emphasize that if you want to find a Jesus story, this is where to look. Remember that all of the information you need is on the bookmarks.

12. Once all the bookmarks have been inserted, continue drilling participants as time allows, locating famous stories and figures in the Bible
from the information provided on the bookmarks. Award prizes (candy,
etc.) for just being in the right section (e.g., Pentateuch, Letters).

13. Encourage participants to continue quizzing themselves at home until
they can remove the bookmarks as they would training wheels—when
they are able to locate famous stories and figures within just a few
minutes by knowing which section to look for. Encourage participants
to show their parents, friends, pastor, etc., how they have learned to
find their way around the Bible with such ease and familiarity.

"I'm trying to get a fresh perspective on scripture."

Annotated Bibliography
for Catholic Scripture Study

Church Teaching

Divino Afflante Spiritu (Pius XII, 1943). In this papal encyclical, which translates as "By the Spirit's Divine Inspiration" and is often called "the charter of Catholic biblical studies," Pope Pius XII urges Catholic biblical scholars to read the Bible according to the literary genre in which each book was written.

Dogmatic Constitution on Divine Revelation—Dei Verbum (Vatican Council II, 1965). Although one of the briefest of the documents issued by the Council, the *Dogmatic Constitution on Divine Revelation* is, at the same time, one of the most important, since it asserts that Scripture and Sacred Tradition form the foundation of the faith. Inspiring. While this document is available in many places, *Vatican Council II: Conciliar and Post Conciliar Documents* edited by Austin Flannery provides an excellent overview of this document and others issued by Vatican Council II.

Besides the Vatican II *Dogmatic Constitution on Divine Revelation*, several other important documents relating to the Bible have come from the Pontifical Biblical Commission (PBC).

Instruction on the Historical Truth of the Gospels (PBC, 1964). This document is the first official Church statement espousing the value of form criticism (see *The Bible Blueprint* page 90). In it, the Biblical Commission explains that the Gospels as we have them today are the result of three stages: Jesus' words as heard by the disciples, the disciples' oral proclamation, and the work of the evangelists. The text may be found in the appendix to Joseph A. Fitzmyer, S.J., *A Christological Catechism: New Testament Answers*. Revised ed. New York: Paulist Press, 1991; pp. 153–64.

Scripture and Christology (PBC, 1984). In this document, the Commission outlines the relationship between biblical interpretation and theology. The text may be found in Joseph A. Fitzmyer, S.J., *Scripture and Christology*. New York: Paulist Press, 1986; pp. 3–53.

The Interpretation of the Bible in the Church (PBC, 1993). This document reviews the key features of various methods of biblical criticism and outlines the characteristics of authentic Catholic interpretation and the interpretation of the Bible in the Church's life. Very practical and clear. The text can be found in *Origins* 23, no. 29 (January 6, 1994): 498–524; also printed as a booklet by St. Paul Books and Media, Boston.

Bibles

The Catholic Study Bible. 2nd ed. New York: Oxford University Press, 2006. Besides the text and notes of the New American Bible with revised New Testament and Psalms, this volume features more than six hundred pages of rich introductory material written by the best of contemporary American Catholic biblical scholars. It includes maps, a glossary, lectionary listings, and more. Valuable for the educated general reader.

The Catholic Bible: Personal Study Edition. 2nd ed. New York: Oxford University Press, 2007. The New American Bible accompanied by simplified versions of the introductory material of The Catholic Study Bible listed above. Good for beginners.

The New Jerusalem Bible. New York: Doubleday, 1999. Excellent contemporary British translation famous for its informative study notes, further enhanced for the second edition. The Old Testament notes surpass those of the current New American Bible. However, note that the less expensive Reader's Edition of the NJB does not contain study notes.

Reference Works

The Collegeville Bible Commentary. 2 vols. Collegeville, MN: Liturgical Press, 1992. Passage-by-passage explanations of each book of the Bible; good for beginners.

The Collegeville Pastoral Dictionary of Biblical Theology. Edited by Carroll Stuhlmueller. Collegeville, MN: Liturgical Press, 1996. Rewarding short studies of key ideas and themes. Each article studies its subject in the context of Scripture, but is made twice as valuable by including a section on the subject as it has been treated in the pastoral and liturgical tradition.

McKenzie, John L. *Dictionary of the Bible.* New York: Touchstone, 1995. Originally published in 1965, this reprint edition is a remarkable, very inexpensive work with short articles on thousands of biblical topics. A steal!

The HarperCollins Bible Dictionary. Edited by Paul J. Achtemeier. San Francisco: HarperCollins, 1996. Short, scholarly articles on a full range of biblical subjects.

Collegeville Bible Commentary series. Collegeville, MN: Liturgical Press, various publication dates. Extensive commentary on books of Scripture from a Catholic perspective by international Scripture scholars, with welcome attention to the history of interpretation by the Church Fathers. Valuable.

The Navarre Bible (Texts and Commentaries), Scepter Publishers, various publication dates. Contains the Revised Standard Version – Catholic Edition, along with the Latin Vulgate Bible and extensive commentary that draws from Church documents and the writings of the Doctors and Fathers of the Church.

The New Jerome Biblical Commentary. Edited by Raymond Brown, Joseph Fitzmyer, and Roland Murphy. Englewood Cliffs, NJ: Prentice Hall, 1999. The preeminent work of Catholic biblical scholarship. For advanced students.

The New World Dictionary-Concordance to the New American Bible. New York: World Publishing, 1982. More of a dictionary than a concordance, but great for beginners.

Sacra Pagina series. Edited by Daniel J. Harrington, SJ. Collegeville, MN: Liturgical Press, various publication dates. Written by an international team of biblical scholars. For advanced students.

Secondary Works

These authors are some of the most well-respected contemporary Catholic theologians. Here are some of their more groundbreaking works.

Alter, Robert. *The Art of Biblical Narrative.* New York: Basic Books, 1981. This and the next volume represent some of the best of modern literary study of Scripture.

_____. *The Art of Biblical Poetry.* New York: Basic Books, 1985. Also very revealing.

Boadt, Lawrence. *Reading the Old Testament: An Introduction.* New York: Paulist Press, 1984. A basic work, very helpful.

Brown, Raymond E. *Biblical Exegesis and Church Doctrine.* New York: Paulist Press, 1985. Short essays exploring traditional Catholic positions such as the virginal conception of Jesus in the light of modern scholarship.

_____. *The Critical Meaning of the Bible.* New York: Paulist Press, 1981. Rewarding essays on the Catholic Church's engagement with critical Scripture scholarship by one of the leading Catholic biblical scholars of our time.

_____. *Introduction to the New Testament.* New York: Doubleday, 1997. Considered by many to be the standard advanced introduction to the New Testament.

_____. *Responses to 101 Questions on the Bible.* New York: Paulist Press, 1990. Question-and-answer style discussion treating common questions. Brown never dodges an issue.

Brueggemann, Walter. *The Bible Makes Sense.* Louisville, KY: Westminster John Knox Press, 2001. Creative and stimulating invitation to read Scripture.

Campbell, James. *The Stories of the Old Testament: A Catholic's Guide.* Chicago: Loyola Press, 2007. Provides the background needed to understand essential Old Testament stories from Genesis to Malachi.

Casey, Michael. *Sacred Reading: The Ancient Art of* Lectio Divina. Liguori, MO: Triumph Books, 1996. An excellent examination of the contemplative approach to praying with Scripture.

Cavalletti, Sofia. *History's Golden Thread: The History of Salvation.* Chicago: Catechesis of the Good Shepherd Publications, 1999. Well-crafted, richly suggestive tracing of typological relations in the Scriptures. Welcome vision of the Old and New Testaments as one Word of God.

Chilson, Richard. *Full Christianity: A Catholic Response to Fundamental Questions.* New York: Paulist Press, 1985. Written well for the general reader, using a question-and-answer format to show the differences between the Catholic and Fundamentalist visions of Christianity.

Days of the Lord: The Liturgical Year. Seven volumes. Collegeville, MN. Liturgical Press, 1991–94. Solid reflections on passages from the lectionary. Translated from French.

Fitzmyer, Joseph A. *A Christological Catechism: New Testament Answers.* Rev. ed. New York: Paulist Press, 1991. Questions and answers on who Jesus was according to the Bible from a Catholic perspective. Includes text of Pontifical Biblical Commission's 1964 *Instruction on the Historical Truth of the Gospels.*

Grant, Robert M., and David Tracy. *A Short History of the Interpretation of the Bible.* 2nd ed. Philadelphia: Fortress Press, 1984. Fascinating panorama of the perspectives and uses to which Scripture has been put. Tracy's section gives a philosophical orientation to contemporary issues in biblical hermeneutics.

Hall, Thelma. *Too Deep for Words: Rediscovering* Lectio Divina. New York: Paulist Press, 1988. Explains *lectio divina* and provides five hundred thematically arranged Scripture texts for prayer.

Harrington, Daniel. *Interpreting the New Testament: A Practical Guide.* Collegeville, MN: Liturgical Press, 1990. First volume of the NT commentary series gives a background to the series and reviews modern methods of New Testament study.

———. *Interpreting the Old Testament: A Practical Guide.* Collegeville, MN: Liturgical Press, 1991. First volume of the OT commentary series gives a background to the series and reviews modern methods of Old Testament study.

Hestenes, Roberta. *Using the Bible in Groups.* Philadelphia: Westminster John Knox Press, 1983. Basics of group studies. Protestant perspective.

Johnson, Luke Timothy. *The Writings of the New Testament: An Introduction.* Rev. ed. Minneapolis: Augsburg Fortress, 1998. Well-written introduction with acute attention to each book's final literary and theological shape. For advanced students.

Kodell, Jerome. *The Catholic Bible Study Handbook.* 2nd rev. ed. Ann Arbor, MI: Charis Books, 2001. Readable book touching on development, background, and approaches to the Bible.

Martin, George. *Reading Scripture as the Word of God.* 4th ed. Ann Arbor, MI: Servant Publications, 1998. Knowledgeable, wise help for approaching a disciplined practice of reading the Scriptures by a gentle guide who discovered the path for himself. Excellent.

Perkins, Pheme. *Reading the New Testament: An Introduction.* Rev. ed. New York: Paulist Press, 1988. Basic introduction to content and themes of the New Testament; strong on historical background.

Books and Their Abbreviations in Biblical Order

Old Testament

Genesis	Gn	Isaiah	Is
Exodus	Ex	Jeremiah	Jer
Leviticus	Lv	Lamentations	Lam
Numbers	Nm	Baruch	Bar
Deuteronomy	Dt	Ezekiel	Ez
Joshua	Jo	Daniel	Dn
Judges	Jgs	Hosea	Hos
Ruth	Ru	Joel	Jl
1 Samuel	1 Sm	Amos	Am
2 Samuel	1 Sm	Obadiah	Ob
1 Kings	1 Kgs	Jonah	Jon
2 Kings	2 Kgs	Micah	Mi
1 Chronicles	1 Chr	Nahum	Na
2 Chronicles	2 Chr	Habakkuk	Hb
Ezra	Ezr	Zephaniah	Zep
Nehemiah	Neh	Haggai	Hg
Tobit	Tb	Zechariah	Zec
Judith	Jdt	Malachi	Mal
Esther	Est		
1 Maccabees	1 Mc		
2 Maccabees	2 Mc		
Job	Jb		
Psalms	Ps		
Proverbs	Prv		
Ecclesiastes	Eccl		
Song of Songs	Sg		
Wisdom	Ws		
Sirach	Sir		

New Testament

Matthew	Mt
Mark	Mk
Luke	Lk
John	Jn
Acts of the Apostles	Acts
Romans	Rom
1 Corinthians	1 Cor
2 Corinthians	2 Cor
Galatians	Gal
Ephesians	Eph
Phillipians	Phil
Colossians	Col
1 Thessalonians	1 Thes
2 Thessalonians	2 Thes
1 Timothy	1 Tm
2 Timothy	2 Tm
Titus	Ti
Philemon	Phlm
Hebrews	Heb
James	Jas
1 Peter	1 Pt
2 Peter	2 Pt
1 John	1 Jn
2 John	2 Jn
3 John	3 Jn
Jude	Jude
Revelation	Rv

Books and Their Abbreviations in Alphabetical Order

Old Testament

Amos	Am	1 Maccabees	1 Mc
Baruch	Bar	2 Maccabees	2 Mc
1 Chronicles	1 Chr	Malachi	Mal
2 Chronicles	2 Chr	Micah	Mi
Daniel	Dn	Nahum	Na
Deuteronomy	Dt	Nehemiah	Neh
Ecclesiastes	Eccl	Numbers	Nm
Esther	Est	Obadiah	Ob
Exodus	Ex	Proverbs	Prv
Ezekiel	Ez	Psalms	Ps
Ezra	Ezr	Ruth	Ru
Genesis	Gn	1 Samuel	1 Sm
Habakkuk	Hb	2 Samuel	2 Sm
Haggai	Hg	Sirach	Sir
Hosea	Hos	Song of Songs	Sg
Isaiah	Is	Tobit	Tb
Jeremiah	Jer	Wisdom	Ws
Job	Jb	Zechariah	Zec
Joel	Jl	Zephaniah	Zep
Jonah	Jon		
Joshua	Jo		
Judges	Jgs		
Judith	Jdt		
1 Kings	1 Kgs		
2 Kings	2 Kgs		
Lamentations	Lam		
Leviticus	Lv		

New Testament

Acts of the Apostles	Acts
Colossians	Col
1 Corinthians	1 Cor
2 Corinthians	2 Cor
Ephesians	Eph
Galatians	Gal
Hebrews	Heb
James	Jas
John (Gospel)	Jn
1 John	1 Jn
2 John	2 Jn
3 John	3 Jn
Jude	Jude
Luke	Lk
Mark	Mk
Matthew	Mt
1 Peter	1 Pt
2 Peter	2 Pt
Philemon	Phlm
Philippians	Phil
Revelation	Rv
Romans	Rom
1 Thessalonians	1 Thes
2 Thessalonians	2 Thes
1 Timothy	1 Tm
2 Timothy	2 Tm
Titus	Ti

Salvation History Timeline

Stories of the Beginning (Prehistory)

Creation
Sin and the Promise
Cain and Abel
The Flood
The Tower of Babel

BC

c. 1850 ▶ Abraham, Our Father in Faith

1800 ▶ The Patriarchs (Isaac, Jacob)

1700

c. 1650 ▶ Joseph sold into slavery

1500

1400

1300

c. 1280 ▶ The Exodus and the Ten Commandments

1200

▶ Judges (Gideon, Samson, Deborah, Samuel)

1100

Kings (Saul)
1000 ▶ David, the Greatest King of Israel

961 ▶ Solomon, Builder of the Temple

900

800

Prophets (Elijah, Isaiah, Amos)
721 ▶ Fall of the Northern Kingdom (Jeremiah)

700

600

587 ▶ Fall of the Southern Kingdom and Exile to
Babylon (Ezekiel, Second Isaiah)

537 ▶ Return to Judah (Third Isaiah)

400

300

200

165 ▶ Maccabean Revolt and Rededication of
the Temple

100

AD ▶ Anno Domini, the Year of Our Lord—
Jesus, the fulfillment of God's plan, is born.

MAP OF HOLY LAND
in the Time of Jesus

Damascus

Tyre

PHOENICIA

Caesarea Philippi

SYRIA

GALILEE
Capernaum
Cana
Bethsaida
Magdala
SEA OF
GALILEE
Nazareth
Nain

Mount
Tabor

M E D I T E R R A N E A N   S E A

Jordan River

DISTRICT of the
TEN CITIES

Samaria
SAMARIA
Shechem
Penuel
Jabbok River
PEREA
Shiloh
Bethel
Emmaus
Jericho
JERUSALEM
Mount of
Olives
Bethlehem
Hebron
DEAD
SEA

JUDEA

Beersheba

MOAB

N

NEGEV

EDOM

0   10   20   30   40   50 Miles

Map of the Holy Land

Map Glossary

Bethlehem is a city five miles south of Jerusalem. David was anointed king of Israel at Bethlehem. Jesus was born in Bethlehem.

Cana was a town located five to nine miles from Nazareth. The Gospel of John tells us that Jesus performed his first miracle at Cana, changing water into wine.

Capernaum was located twenty-three miles from Nazareth on the northern shore of the Sea of Galilee. Jesus lived in Capernaum and began his ministry there.

Galilee is the northern region of Palestine. It has hills and fertile plains. Most events in the Gospels of Matthew, Mark, and Luke occurred in Galilee.

Jerusalem is located in the southern part of Palestine and is the capital city of Israel. The city contains sites that are holy to Jews, Christians, and Muslims. The great Temple, long the center of the Israelites' religion, was located in Jerusalem.

Jordan River is a long, curving river in Palestine. John the Baptist baptized Jesus in the Jordan River.

Judea was the southern region of Palestine in Greek and Roman times. Bethlehem and Jersusalem were both located in Judea.

Nazareth is the city where Jesus lived with his parents, Mary and Joseph, before his public ministry.

Palestine is the area of land on the eastern shore of the Mediterranean Sea that includes parts of what is today Egypt, Israel, and Jordan. Palestine is often called the Holy Land because it has religious significance for Jews, Christians, and Muslims.

Bibliography

Bergant, Dianne. *Introduction to the Bible.* Collegeville Bible Commentary: Old Testament 1. Collegeville, MN: Liturgical Press, 1985.

Brown, Raymond E., Joseph A. Fitzmeyer, and Roland E. Murphy, eds. *The Jerome Biblical Commentary.* Englewood Cliffs, NJ: Prentice Hall, 1968.

The Catholic Study Bible: New American Bible. New York: Oxford University Press, 1990.

Charpentier, Etienne. *How to Read the Old Testament.* Translated by John Bowden. New York: Crossroad, 1982.

The Complete Parallel Bible with the Apocryphal/Deuterocanonical Books: New Revised Standard Version, Revised English Bible, New American Bible, New Jerusalem Bible. New York: Oxford University Press, 1993.

Flannery, Austin, ed. *Vatican Council II.* Vol. 1, *The Conciliar and Post Conciliar Documents.* Rev. ed. Northport, NY: Costello, 1975.

Ludwig, Robert A. *Reconstructing Catholicism: For a New Generation.* New York: Crossroad, 1995.

Pontifical Biblical Commission. "The Interpretation of the Bible in the Church." *Origins* 23, no. 29 (January 6, 1994): 498–524.

Rolheiser, Ronald. *Against an Infinite Horizon: The Finger of God in Our Everyday Lives.* Rev. ed. New York: Crossroad, 2001.

Witherington, Ben. *Conflict and Community in Corinth: A Socio-Rhetorical Commentary on 1 and 2 Corinthians.* Grand Rapids, MI: Wm. B. Eerdmans, 1995.

Author Biography

Joe Paprocki, DMin, is National Consultant for Faith Formation at Loyola Press in Chicago. Joe has over thirty years of experience in pastoral ministry in the Archdiocese of Chicago. He is the author of numerous books on pastoral ministry and catechesis, including the best sellers *A Well-Built Faith* and *The Catechist's Toolbox.* Currently an eighth-grade catechist, Joe blogs about his catechetical experiences at www.catechistsjourney.com.

More pertinent tips and practical teaching from Joe Paprocki . . .

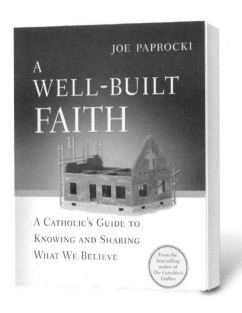

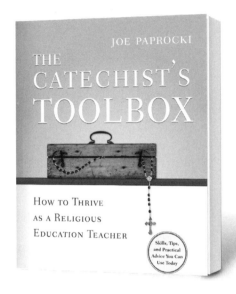

A Well-Built Faith
A Catholic's Guide to Knowing and Sharing What We Believe

ISBN-13: 978-0-8294-2757-8
2008 • Pb • 176 pgs • $9.95

From the Trinity to the seven sacraments, from the Ten Commandments to the Gifts of the Holy Spirit, *A Well-Built Faith* helps Catholics know the facts of their faith.

The Catechist's Toolbox
How to Thrive as a Religious Education Teacher

ISBN-13: 978-0-8294-2451-5
2007 • Pb • 152 pgs • $9.95

The Catechist's Toolbox is an invaluable collection of methodologies, techniques, and tips that provide on-the-job training for any new catechist. Essential catechist skills are taught throughout this best-selling book.

Leader Guides are also available for both books!

Available wherever books are sold, including **www.loyolapress.com/store**